COUNTRY CHAFF II

by Jerry Easterling

West Side
Publishing Co.
1127 Edgewater NW
Salem, OR 97304

Production by West Side Publishing Co.

Illustrations and cover design by Kristi Gilman

Cover Photo by Gerry Lewin

ISBN 0-944540-03-1

Library of Congress Catalog Card Number: 87-51280

To Susan, Steve and Leith,
who make being a father easy

Preface

Reading a Jerry Easterling story is like taking a drink of water from a cold mountain brook; or standing in the crisp silence of a dew-fresh country morning; or getting a surprise hug from a loved one. And sometimes you just plain laugh out loud at his wry observations, which makes you feel better in spite of yourself.

In this, Easterling's second collection of columns written for the Salem, Ore., Statesman-Journal, all the elements that combined to make the first "Country Chaff" a success are there: the spare and graceful writing style; the understated humor; the ability to select a plain pebble from under the feet of our hurried lives, polish it and show us the gem we should have seen in the first place. He gives us a second chance to look and appreciate.

"Country Chaff II" starts off with Jerry's national award-winning story, "Farewell to Joy," a chronicle of his family's exodus from the Dust Bowl-cursed Nebraska of the 1930s. Although it's only three pages long, the story packs a novel within it, and is as fine a piece of writing as anything Steinbeck did on the same subject.

Easterling then continues to enthrall with tales of his family and friends, acquaintances, events; of bouts with electricity and postholes, people and critters; the beautiful and the unsavory; and he asks such questions as why chickens, with "their brains all scrunched up like that," are smart enough to pick just the right time to scratch up two rows of newly planted petunias.

Welcome again, then, to the world of Jerry Easterling's "Country Chaff," a world we all share regardless of our experience or position. I know you will enjoy reading the book as much as I have enjoyed editing and publishing it.

Tim Hinshaw
West Side Publishing Co.

Table of Contents

THE FLAVOR OF LIFE

Nebraska: 1936

Farewell To Joy

At odd times, in strange places, I think about it.

When I see wind rippling grass in dark green fields, it comes back to me. When I watch clear running water, and sprinklers firing salvos into the sun, I see it again.

Rain makes me remember. And the wind. Long, dark, moist furrows -- freshly plowed -- bring it all back, and the rich, thick, musty smells of harvest.

In contrast they make it all so vivid: the Great Plains -- the 1930s -- and the drought.

And the dust: always the dust, rising and swirling, forever shifting.

And the wind that created it: a nervous prowler, sweeping across the prairies like a dark, relentless demon. And dust hanging wearily in the air when it sometimes halted, tired clouds looking for a place to rest.

But there was no rest. The wind returned. Day after day it came back. It couldn't ignore the 450,000 square miles of dusty playground the Dust Bowl became when the drought descended upon it.

It came slyly, in great stillness, as intruders often do. I remember the strange hush that settled over the vast corn fields near the road my sorrel pony Joy and I were following. We were going home from school, where she spent the day with other ponies in a small barn while classes were in session. It was 1932.

We were three miles east of Kearney, Nebraska. We were going south, toward the farm my folks owned near the Platte River two miles farther on. It was an afternoon in the fall, and nothing stirred, not even the faded leaves that hung from the willows growing along the ditches.

In the silence I could feel tension, like a force being contained against its will. Joy could feel it too. She flicked her ears uneasily, and swung her head from side to side. There was a peculiar thrumming in the air, the sound that no sound makes.

In the corn fields great flocks of ducks and geese had taken refuge. During their long southerly migration in the fall, the Great Plains became their breadbasket. The fields supplied the fuel that kept the big birds pumping across mile after mile of deep curving sky that ended on the straight, flat line of the horizon.

They, too, sensed something. They ballooned up out of the fields in flurries, then settled back down again. They were fearful and confused. They flew low. In the sky they sensed a danger that being on the ground did not allay.

The clouds had been indistinct, a haze on the horizon, but soon they began taking shape. Slowly, like a towering range of mountains, they advanced upon us. As they drew near, huge billowy peaks loomed over us. They were clouds such as I had never seen before. When I touched her with my heels, Joy broke into a full gallop. She was also worried.

The storm struck late that afternoon, just after we got home. The wind announced its arrival with a roar, and everything went dark. Dust filled the air, and we blindly groped around. In an instant, daylight had disappeared.

The Great Plains were on the move. The dust we breathed had come from farms in Texas, Oklahoma and Kansas. The next day the Dakotas got a taste of Nebraska.

The dust came to stay. It filled everything, and tainted all. It seeped into the houses, the food, the water. With wet cloths Mother tried to seal around the doors and windows. When that failed, we used the cloths as masks to filter it out of our breath.

Landmarks blurred. Everything ran together in murky vagueness. At times we couldn't see the ground in front of our feet.

The drought was the fault of men, the experts claimed, men who upset the fragile balance of things. With their plows, they said, farmers set the Great Plains free when they rooted out the native grasses with which nature had controlled them.

When moisture was sufficient, they kept the land in place with crops. But when the rains no longer came, and nothing grew, dust rose up like an eager host to greet the wind.

But people persisted. They continued to plant, and watched their labors go up in dust. Some seeds never sprouted. Those that did soon died in the hot, dry fields and their tattered leaves rustled in the wind. Livestock grew lean and gaunt as dust formed like goggles around their eyes.

That's the way our cows began to look. And they didn't milk as well because feed was short. The land had rebelled.

I can still see them: the cows, humped up in the wind with their heads down, still as dusty paintings. I can still hear them bawling wearily as they waited like dusky phantoms in the corral.

The relentless wind was an artful sculptor. It rippled the fields with soft, dusty dunes, and buried the fences in long smooth swells. With an artistic flourish, it laid dark wreaths upon a dying land.

For many it was a time to leave, a time to search for more promising places. Among the searchers were my folks. And we were luckier than lots of families. We were rich compared to those in Texas and Oklahoma who had nothing to take when they got ready to leave.

I have before me a sale bill dated Tuesday, November 1, 1936:

"As I am leaving the state," it says, "I will sell my personal property at Public Auction at my farm...

"Sale starts at 1 o'clock," and "Barney Shepers Lunch Wagon on the ground."

Bob Easterling was the owner and W. W. Wimberly was the auctioneer. The clerk was Lloyd Ferrell.

November 1, 1936, was a raw windy day, and those who came to the sale huddled up in their coats and didn't say much. They didn't bid much either. They couldn't. The pockets they shoved their hands into were about as empty as they could get.

I rode Joy around the ring of silent, sober faces to show that she was sound as Col. Wimberly sold her. Then I rode her back into the barn and tied her up. After I had hugged her hard around the neck, I ran out into the waiting wind.

The next day we started west.

PUBLISHER'S NOTE: The preceding story, "Farewell To Joy," was honored as first place winner in the Best of Gannett competition among the newspaper chain's many dailies across the nation.

"Farewell To Joy" first appeared as a column in the Salem, Oregon Statesman-Journal under the title, "Erosion."

Memory Makers

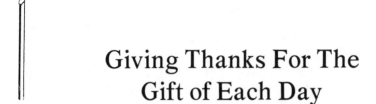

Giving Thanks For The Gift of Each Day

Not until the years have flowed together in a grey, listless haze do we realize that days are treasures that we shouldn't have frittered away. I'm reminded of that on this Thanksgiving Day by another Thanksgiving from a long time ago.

I've wasted a lot of time -- as much as anyone, I suppose. But since then I haven't been able to do so without feeling a little guilty.

We had just arrived in Oregon from Nebraska. I was 11, and I could hardly believe what I was seeing. It was so green, and warm and pretty. Where was the wind, I wondered, that had churned the Great Plains into a dusty bowl?

My dreams of living in the West were finally coming true. And they were fresh and bright and shiny, even after a 2,000 mile ride. From the back seat of the car I had looked at them a thousand times a day.

Oregon dazzled me. Its mountains were overwhelming, and great green forests stretched farther than any dream could reach. For the first time I saw deer, and silver grey squirrels -- and squirrels that soared like gliders.

Grouse exploded among the underbrush and sailed like bullets through the trees. The bear I met tingled hair upon my neck as we both took off in fright. And once I heard a cougar squall.

I met Daniel Boone on magic afternoons as he came swinging over a ridge with his rifle swinging loosely in his hand. In forests that have long since disappeared, brave men struggled against great odds in lively imaginations. On wooded slopes, history came alive.

A one-room school sat on a hill not far from the farm my folks had leased. It was tall and square and spare, without frill of any kind. No lesson there was ever dolled up in educational fluff to make it easier to absorb.

New places, and new faces. And kids who hadn't the faintest idea where I was from, and had no desire to find out. Kids who said, "You talk funny."

They did too, but when I told them so they scoffed. It didn't make much difference, though, because we laughed alike when we were happy, and cried alike when we were sad. When it became important, we all knew how to feel.

We arrived in the fall, and soon the winter rains began. They came with a whoosh of wind that aroused memories of the Great Plains, but it wasn't an ill wind with a dirty, dusty breath.

The rain came in the night and I listened from an upstairs bedroom as it purred softly on the roof like a big, contented cat. It made a peaceful sound, the kind that dreams take pleasure in.

Soon the ditches filled with water, and each became a risky river to cross, a mighty torrent to tame. Lower fields filled with water, and we splashed in the lakes that they became.

On a hill behind the house a forest of tall, straight firs stood. And in the evening, when dusk was coming down, they dripped softly in the rain, sadly, like mourners grieving.

Mother said it would be different when we moved, and it was. Thanksgiving was different, too. For the the first time we were alone: my mother, my dad, my brother, my sister and me. But the sun cheered us on that special day, and the air was clear and clean.

After dinner we walked in the field south of the house, and circled slowly through the little orchard that grew on the slope below the fence. The sun smiled and it was warm.

I sensed it then. And I know with certainty that every day is a gift that each of us wraps in our own peculiar way before we consign it to the past. And only we can keep it from becoming a hazy, listless grey.

The choice is ours, and for that we should be thankful.

Sooty Lamp Makes The Memories Shine

An old kerosene lamp sits as a centerpiece on our kitchen table. When I lit it the other night, after the electricity had gone off, memories came flickering back to life.

As I watched that uneasy little crescent of flame, I had trouble believing that we once depended upon lamps for all our light at night.

They produced a weak, anemic glow. It wasn't bright at all. A firefly with a dead cell could have done as well.

By their feeble light my brother, my sister and I did our homework, as we hunched up over the rim of the kitchen table. To make them as bright as possible we turned the wick up as high as we dared.

But it was a temporary benefit. Within minutes the lamp would begin to smoke and the light would dim as the chimney loaded up with soot.

When I was small and didn't know any better, my brother told me to take a chimney off one night and clean it.

He didn't tell me how hot chimneys got and it fried my fingers to a crisp. It had just cleared the four metal arms that held it when I let it fall.

It broke when it hit the floor and my brother said: "You shouldn't a let it go." If he hadn't been bigger than I was -- and four years older -- I would have busted his chimney then and there.

We didn't have another one, and wouldn't have until Dad went to town. So we studied nearly a week without a chimney on the lamp, and it was sort of interesting.

With no chimney to stabilize it, the light flickered freely. After a while it seemed that everything was undulating slowly, the ways things do that ripple in and out of focus under water.

It provided a source of entertainment Dad and Mother hadn't foreseen. The light turned the shadowy silhouettes we formed with our hands into wild beasts that cavorted crazily on the walls.

The shadows provided an exciting world of fantasy that homework couldn't compete with. When my brother's hands were a dark dog snapping at the dusky rabbit my sister's fingers had become, two-plus-two didn't stand a chance.

When we tired of that, it was time to complain of eyestrain. It didn't work often, but it did occasionally. And nothing did more for morale than an imaginary ailment that got us out of something we didn't want to do.

But there is nothing imaginary about the way I feel when the electricity goes off and we have to rely on that coal-oil lamp again.

When I flip a switch and nothing lights up I sympathize with Jonah, who didn't have so much as an electric eel to light his way while in the belly of the whale.

When my prayers were answered the other night, and the lights came on again, I thanked old Ben Franklin for flying his kite on that dark and stormy night. If he hadn't discovered electricity, I would never have forgiven him.

Children Know No Bias

My mother was born on a midwestern farm in 1900. When she was a little girl her father owned a rotary corn grinder that was powered by horses that walked in circles around it.

While playing one day, her foot was badly bruised by the tongue the horses were hitched to. While it was healing, her mother restricted her to the house so she wouldn't injure it again.

Soon after that a team of horses swung into her father's farm pulling a wagon on which a small house had been built. It was a horse trader traveling with his wife and daughter. Tied to the back end of the wagon was a string of horses.

In those days that was common. Horse traders made their living traveling around the country. And after they had done all the wheeling and dealing they could in one part of the country they moved on to another.

Some were shysters. They would sell any old rack of bones for a sound horse if they thought they could get away with it. And they never traveled the same route twice because they knew someone would be lying in wait for them.

As a consequence, all horse traders were under suspicion. And the honest ones had to overcome the stigma the dishonest ones saddled them with.

When they traveled, they tried to find a friendly farmer who would allow them to pull in for a few days and rest. But the one that stopped while mother was recuperating had a more urgent reason.

His little girl was sick, he said, and he wanted to know if he could camp down by the windmill in the pasture so they would be near water. They would only stay until the little girl was better, he told mother's father.

Only because he felt sorry for the little girl did he allow them to. Under normal circumstances he would have told the trader to keep on going.

My mother and her twin brother Bernard were told not to go near them "because they are horse traders." The way their mother said "horse traders" left no doubt about the shady nature of their character.

Since childish curiosity cannot be satisfied at a distance, Bernard sneaked off one day to see them. And the little girl who would become my mother waited anxiously for his report. Why, she wondered, was he staying so long? She was getting worried.

When Bernard finally returned he told her he had stayed so long because they were so nice. "And she puts out a real clean wash," he said, "and she sure does bake good bread."

They sounded like such fine folks mother couldn't wait to meet them. So the next day she and Bernard both slipped off for a visit. And it was slow going because mother was still hobbling on her sore foot.

All of her life, she remembered how nicely she and Bernard were treated. And she discovered his report about the wash was true. And the lady really did bake good bread. And, of course, they stayed longer than they intended to.

On their way home their luck ran out because mother couldn't travel fast enough. They were apprehended by their mother, who had been looking for them, and she wasn't very happy.

But when they told her how nice the people were -- and how cute the little girl was -- their mother finally consented to go see them. And after visiting with them, she agreed. "They are real nice folks," she said.

The horse trader and his family stayed a few more days down in the pasture, mother said, then they moved on and she never heard from them again.

But for a moment they had touched each other. And little children had led the way because they didn't know that the path to the windmill was imperiled by prejudice.

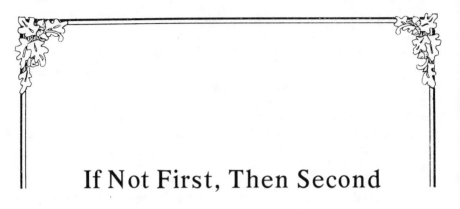

If Not First, Then Second

I made one foray into horse racing. It was my last. I was just a kid, but I remember it like it was yesterday. I guess the things you really hang your hopes on stick the longest in your mind when they go sour.

I planned and planned. I waited and waited for that little Nebraska county fair to open, but time seemed to stand still. If it would slow down now like it did then, I would live to be 500 years old. But that's the way it is when you're eight or nine, and you're going to win all that money as you come thundering down to the wire leading the pack.

I said I made a foray into horse racing. But that isn't quite right. My horse was a pony. She was light tan in color with a flaxen mane and tail. She had four white stockings, and a blaze on her face. I called her Joy. And she could run.

As the day approached, my nerves began acting up. I would wake up in the middle of the night with the shivers. I imagined all kinds of things happening, but never once did I think about it raining. That is something it had quit doing in Nebraska during the Dust Bowl years. But rain it did. Not much, but enough to postpone for one day the debut Joy and I were going to make.

So I spent another sleepless night, and prayed for a clear day. My prayers were answered. It quit raining -- and it didn't rain again for seven years.

The next morning we loaded Joy in the trailer and took off for town. It was an unnerving experience for her. She was a country pony. Even though that little Nebraska town wasn't much of a city in those days, it was different than anything she was used to. By the time we got to the fairgrounds, she was pretty excited.

To make matters worse, the race was delayed. A daredevil riding a motorcycle was going to make a running jump off a ramp, but the ramp broke. The crowd loved it as he and the motorcycle went cartwheeling through the air, but he didn't. The motorcycle came down on top of him, and

11

he didn't get up. It was at least 30 minutes before the racetrack where he had been performing was cleared of debris.

But the moment arrived -- at last. And I had never seen so many ponies in my life. None compared to Joy, of course, but it looked as if every kid in the country had dreams of galloping off with the big money.

Joy was flicking her ears, and the whites of her eyes were showing as I led her out on the track and mounted. I scratched her neck, and talked to her as we approached the starting line. She cocked one ear back to listen, but she was tossing her head nervously as we cantered into place. It was plain to see that my dreams of fame were not shared by her.

It was quite a race. For a while Joy and I had the track all to ourselves. We had the field all to ourselves because she whirled at the sound of the starting gun and began running in the opposite direction. I can well remember the snicker that went up from the crowd. By the time I got her turned around, my dream of fame and fortune had been scalded in shame.

But Joy could run. And when she lined out the second time, she lined out in earnest. She seemed to flatten out as she picked up speed. It seemed that in one grand effort she was trying to redeem herself. When she was running hard she didn't jar the way most horses do. She rippled like water.

Despite the wrong-way start, she rippled right on through that herd of ponies and finished second.

By present standards we didn't win much for second place. I think it was $1.50, but it was a lot of money for a kid in those days. I didn't think Joy had done too badly.

She hadn't won. But she had placed, and she had put on quite a show. I was proud of her. And I knew that if she hadn't got her directions mixed up we would have run off and left them all in the dust that was beginning to blow again as we headed for home.

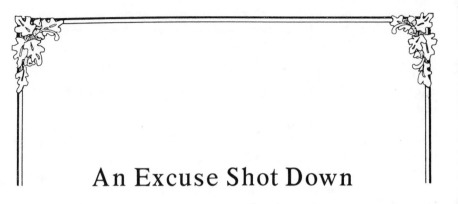

An Excuse Shot Down

When I was 13 or so, I hunted a lot. That was before the great westward rush of people after World War II, and the Coast Range Mountains were truly a wilderness. You could travel for miles and never see another person. There were no fences, and few roads. The trails found there were made by deer. It was a Paradise.

Sometimes I hunted alone, but I preferred to hunt with another kid about my age, who had been born and raised in the mountains. His knowledge of plants and animals amazed me. If Tim had been born 100 years earlier, he would have been a mountain man. He could see things I could stare at for 10 minutes and still not see. No sound escaped him. He heard even the slightest rustle in the brush, and knew what it meant.

He was ingenious in the way that people are who have to rely upon themselves for the things they get. With hardly any tools at all, he could fix nearly anything.

If the firing pin in his rifle went haywire, he would rummage around until he found a piece of iron, then file it down to size. He was always tinkering with an old gun he had traded for -- and when he was through tinkering it usually fired.

Tim was a good hunter, much better than I was, and he was fun to be with. I never saw him mad. He accepted things as they were, and laughed along the way. He was a free spirit. He belonged to the mountains, and they belonged to him. From him, they didn't hide their secrets.

There was only one problem. My folks didn't think much of Tim. They thought he was a ne'er-do-well. Keep fooling around with him, they told me, and you'll never amount to a hill of beans. Since I didn't care about amounting to anything -- not even a hill of beans -- I couldn't understand their concern. I argued, but it did no good. Finally, they forbid me to see him at all. But I didn't.

As soon as I was out of sight, I would start climbing the hills toward an old clearing where we sometimes met. Or I would go left, and we would meet at the old stump next to the creek where the water swirled in a big pool. If anything, intrigue and deception made hunting even more exciting.

But the day Tim shot a grouse was the day my goose was cooked, so to speak. I didn't want to, but he insisted that I take it home.

"I'll get another one," he said. "There's lots of them still out there." He was being generous, and I didn't want to disappoint him. With the grouse tied to my belt, I started home.

Before I took it in to Mother, I cleaned it. That surprised her, because it wasn't something I did often. She decided that we should have it for dinner the next day. I took a deep breath and hoped for the best.

When we sat down for dinner the next day, I wasn't too hungry. As the plate of grouse was passed around, a covey of butterflies fluttered in my stomach. I couldn't understand why I had gotten into such a mess.

By the time we were half way through the meal most of the grouse was gone, and I was beginning to think that the Man upstairs was on my side. But I knew I was mistaken when Dad suddenly stopped eating and slowly leaned back in his chair. I could feel his eyes on me as I leaned over my plate. As I waited, my heart picked up speed.

"What's that?" he asked, as he held out his hand.

I glanced up and shook my head. "I don't know," I said.

"Then I'll tell you what it is," he said. "That's a shot from a shotgun shell."

I stared down at my hands as everyone's eyes settled on me and the silence got bigger and bigger.

"Since you were hunting with a .22," Dad said, "how do you explain this?"

I didn't have to. Everyone knew that grouse had been shot with Tim's shotgun -- and I knew my time was coming.

I haven't hunted for years. Somewhere along the line, I lost the desire. I'm not sure, but it wouldn't surprise me if that grouse had a lot to do with my loss of interest.

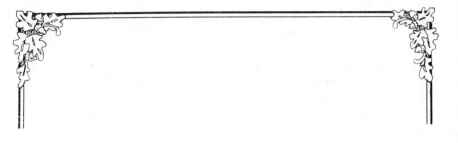

An Education That Works

I had it all mapped out. I would quit school. It was too dull and boring to interfere with the exciting things I wanted to do. There was a big, wide world out there and I wanted to see it all.

I was a sophomore in high school, and suddenly I had become very smart. Almost overnight, it seemed, I had come into possession of vast wisdom. It was almost infinite. I had all the answers.

But I ran into a snag. Dad had other ideas, and usually I altered mine so they conformed to his. This time I didn't intend to. I was determined to end my high school education.

If I goofed off often enough -- and fouled up frequently enough -- I figured one of two things would happen: I would either get kicked out of school or Dad would decide I was wasting time and money by being there.

George Paul was the principal of the high school. I don't know why he didn't kick me out. He had every reason to. I worked much harder at being obnoxious than I had ever worked as a student. Finally, I decided he and Dad were in cahoots, and despite everything I did they were going to keep me in school.

Then a strange thing happened. I did as I pleased and no one seemed to care. I skipped school and no one said much of anything. It seemed like I had the best of all possible worlds.

But my smug contentment ended when Dad abruptly came around to my point of view. Since I wasn't learning anything, he decided there wasn't any reason to stay in school.

He told me that on Thursday. Friday, he said, would be my last day. He advised me not to make any plans for the weekend. "I've got a few things lined up for you," he said.

On Saturday morning he put me to work clearing brush along a creek. When I stopped to wipe the sweat out of my eyes, the creek seemed to stretch on and on like the Mississippi River. I could tell by the blisters on my hand that Dad was serious.

And that was just the beginning. I still had the horses to feed and the hogs to slop. As the things Dad insisted upon me doing multiplied, the exciting world I envisioned began to shrivel up in drudgery.

It was early spring, and after we had plowed a field near the creek that I had been clearing of brush, it was up to me to harrow it. And so early one Monday morning there I was.

It was beautiful. The sun was bright, the air was fresh and the birds were singing. It was time for adventure, and I was tramping through plowed ground behind a team of pokey old horses that weren't enjoying themselves any more than I was.

Harrowing is a boring job, and as I stomped along I couldn't help thinking about how bleak my future looked. All I could see was a long narrow tunnel that darkened into a tiny black dot way off in the distance.

To take my mind off such a dismal prospect, I started trying to ride the harrow. By balancing on one of the rails that the teeth were fastened to I could save a step or two.

When my foot slipped, the fun ended. Before I could get the horses stopped it was twisted back under the harrow. As I hobbled through the rest of the day, the great wisdom that I had possessed a week earlier began to dissolve.

One evening after that happened, Dad said Mr. Paul had paid him a visit. Mr. Paul wanted him to let me go back to school, he said. What, he wondered, did I think of that? I thought it was such a good idea, I didn't utter one word of dissent.

They had helped me outsmart myself, but I didn't realize it until later. I never got around to thanking Mr. Paul for what he did, and I'm sorry. If he's still living, I do now.

Fantasy Flies By Night

Before TV settled permanently into American living rooms, movies provided escape into fantasyland. Good and evil fought it out on big silvery screens.

If half the shots fired had hit their mark in westerns, there wouldn't have been enough people left in Hollywood during the 1930s to play a game of croquet.

It's no wonder the screen in those old theaters darkened around the edges and turned brown. Exposure to all that gunsmoke eventually took its toll.

They were great mythical figures, those white-hatted heroes who rode hellbent for election down those twisty trails into the past. Buck Jones and Ken Maynard still stir up little puffs of dust in my memory. So do Bob Steele and Hoot Gibson.

And those serials, those never-ending sagas that went on week after week, were nerve-racking, torturous ordeals. Each segment ended with the hero in such dire straits we could hardly wait a week to see if he had survived.

He always did. With six-guns blazing he would shoot half a dozen outlaws into Boot Hill before he rescued the dewy-eyed heroine, the fairest maiden in all the land. High adventure was highest when it was serialized.

I can still feel the excitement, the breath-taking suspense as Bob Steele raced lickety split for the edge of a cliff he couldn't see in the dark of a frightening night.

The edge of the seats in those old theaters wore out first for good reason. There was no other place to sit when the grim, whiskery villains were waiting to dry gulch the hero as he came riding around the bend.

But relief flared like a campfire in the wind as hundreds of spell-bound eyes watched the culprits, the dirty varmints, slink off to jail after justice had been done.

Movies were made for the night, not the day. That, at least, was the way I

17

felt about them. I think I only saw one matinee when I was a kid because we lived out of town and usually went to the show on Saturday night. And that was enough.

It was a hot day, I remember, and I felt strange going into a theater at high noon. It seemed that I was getting the cart before the horse. Eating breakfast at suppertime was the way it made me feel.

But unease subsided quickly when the action on the screen began. There wasn't room for anything but the suspense that was building in my mind like a balloon about to explode.

My palms were sweaty from hanging on to the back of the seat in front of me as the show came to an end. But when I stepped out of the darkened theater into the hot, mid-afternoon sun, I felt as if I had been betrayed.

The excitement, the heroic fantasies I'd left my seat with vanished as I watched people walk listlessly along the sidewalks. The white-hatted defenders of law and order wilted in the heat, and their horses grew dim as mirages in the desert and disappeared.

Everything was so humdrum, so without flash or fire. I decided then I never wanted to see another daytime movie. The images they aroused couldn't exist in reality's harsh light, and I didn't want to see them die in vain.

Only in darkness could they flourish. There, in soft, satiny light, they could gallop with headlong gallantry through my imagination without taint or tarnish.

Courage reared impatiently then as it waited for evil to make its sly and shifty-eyed debut. Bravery could gleam as bright as the pearl handles on Buck Jones' revolvers in the dark, and chivalry could be the graceful, sweeping arc of his hat as he greeted his lady fair.

Movies made my nights feel safe. With all that courage to draw upon, with all that bravery stiffening a spine that sagged at the sound of a hooting owl, the demons of the dark didn't stand a chance.

Fear of darkness was not a gang of threatening ghosts and ghouls then. It was but a mouse that Buck Jones helped me keep at bay.

Coming Home To Freedom

The day I left it was cold and windy. It was in the fall, and clouds sailed across the sky like raggedy patches of dark gray flannel. It wasn't the best day to begin a trip around the world.

I was 15 and for weeks I had saved. I had the grand total of $6.50 in my pocket when I stepped out on the road and raised my thumb. But no one seemed to notice. As the cars whipped by, I began to shiver.

Finally a truck from the U.S. Forest Service stopped. Canvas stretched over bows covered the bed, and that is where I rode with a crew of workers coming in from the hills. It was warmer there, even if the accommodations weren't first class.

For about 50 miles I rode the truck. When I crawled out it was the middle of the afternoon, and visions of those far-off exotic places that had kept my spirits up earlier were beginning to look a little pale and anemic. They didn't glow with the same bright colors that had made them so appealing a few hours before.

But I was fortunate. Another truck soon came along and picked me up. The driver was a nice guy, but he thought I was a little nutty starting out to see the world that late in the year. And he also surmised that I had left home without telling anyone.

"If I were you," he said, "I would turn around and head back. You got lots of time to see the world."

I shook my head. My pride was at stake. If I didn't keep going I knew I would hate myself in the morning. By then the sky was clouded over, and dusk was beginning to smudge everything with a smeary look. Lights were coming on in the houses along the way, and as I watched them slip by something caught in my throat.

When the driver let me off down on the waterfront it was dark. From across the bay came the low, throaty bellow of a ship heading out to sea. I didn't know anything could sound so forlorn. It opened up a big lonesome hollow in my stomach that regret, remorse and guilt rushed in to fill.

I started walking toward some boxcars standing on rails that came from everywhere. Never had I seen so many tracks. I had no idea there were so many places to go.

I crawled into an empty boxcar and sat down. I was hungry, but I was afraid to leave. I had no idea where I was, nor any idea where anything else was. I decided I would wait until morning before I made a move. And I prayed that the Southern Pacific wouldn't pull the car I was in out to some distant desert siding in Eastern Oregon and forget that it was there.

I was feeling about as low as I could get when I was disturbed by a barking dog. I crawled over to the door and peeked out. Just below was a big police dog. When he saw me he began throwing a fit. I finally found a small piece of 2x4 and threw it at him just as a railroad detective came around the end of the car. I surrendered without a fight.

As we walked toward a small building where there was a telephone, the dog followed me. We had just about reached the door when he grabbed me by the back of the leg. I let out a yell, and the detective made a grab for me. He thought I was trying to get away. He didn't know how happy I was that he had captured me.

There was blood on my leg, and he was genuinely surprised. He looked at the dog and shook his head. "He never did that before," he said. "For some reason he doesn't like you." Then he called the cops.

I spent that night in jail. As I sat there nursing my dog bite, I made an important discovery. I realized that nothing I could ever gain would be worth the price if it cost me my freedom.

And so many sell theirs cheaply. And in so many different ways.

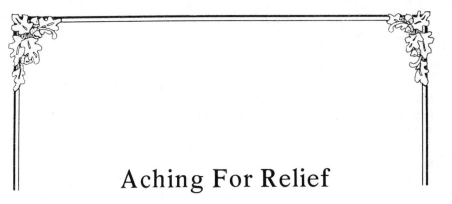

Aching For Relief

By then Dad was a physical wreck. Several serious illnesses plus three major operations had taken their toll. And all those years of smoking had just about ruined his lungs.

But he loved life. And he didn't want to think about the alternative because he figured eternity would get mighty boring after two or three centuries.

"Maybe sooner," he'd say, with an unrepentant grin.

He hadn't taken any better care of his teeth than he had anything else, and the few he had left were dark and decayed. Occasionally one of them would give him fits, but he would tough it out because he didn't want "to go to no damned dentist."

After a night or so the pain would let up, and he would forget about it until the next time. That worked okay until the night all of them decided to ache at once.

For one day and night he put up with them. Then he decided to get them pulled. "If all they're going to do is raise hell," he said, "they can raise hell somewhere else."

He hadn't been to a dentist in years, so he picked one at random out of the telephone directory and gave him a ring. The dentist agreed to see him that afternoon.

I offered to take him, but Dad shook his head. He said he "didn't need no nursemaid" to lead him around. He crawled behind the wheel of his car and stuck a big cigar in his mouth.

"Yeah," he said, "I'll give you a call if I need help."

The dentist had an office about 10 miles away. If he got in on time, we knew Dad wouldn't be there long. About all that was holding his teeth were those twitching, inflamed nerves.

He didn't return when we thought he should, so we called the dentist. He said Dad had left without getting his teeth pulled. The dentist had refused to take them out.

He said Dad was old, his heart was weak, and so were his lungs. The dentist decided that he should go where emergency lifesaving equipment was available in case it became too much of an ordeal for him. He didn't have any idea where Dad had gone.

We were getting ready to look for him when we saw him driving down the road. He always drove faster than he should have, and we figured he was in pretty good shape because he hadn't slowed down.

After he pulled in under the apple tree where he parked, he pushed the door open and swiveled around on the seat so he could spit between his knees.

"Well, by God," he said, "they're gone."

After the dentist had refused to pull his teeth, Dad found another one well past retirement age on a back street in a small, neighboring town. He took one look at him, Dad said, and asked if he thought he could live through it. "I intend to," Dad had told him.

"What if you decide to check out while I'm working on you? Is your family going to sue me?"

"They'll probably give you a medal," Dad said.

Without further ado the old dentist had yanked them out. And Dad had survived. Except for a numbness in his jaw that caused him to lisp a little, he seemed to be in pretty good shape.

Those two -- the old dentist and my dad -- had come a long way down life's twisted road to meet in that shabby, second-story office. And they had admired each other's brash disregard for consequences.

"Hell," said Dad, "nothing that could have happened would have been worse than four teeth aching at once."

There was one thing about him: he had his priorities straight.

A Desire To See
What Mother Saw

Mother died in 1985, and during a sleepless night recently I tried to determine how much influence she'd had upon my life.

I couldn't, of course, because men never know the effect their mothers have upon them. But this I knew for sure: she had offered much more than I had been kind enough to accept.

It is all so obvious now. And in the dark of night, without distraction, I saw more vividly than ever before the gifts she had quietly offered me.

It was there in the softness of her eyes, and the gentless of her smile when she was pleased. And she often was because she knew there was more to life than we ever learn to appreciate. She saw where I was blind.

To her a bird was a source of delight. So was a flower. Dew sparkling in the grass was a field of jewels that money could not buy. Each new day was an adventure.

In an old pair of shoes she traced the history of the child. In an antique bedspread she saw a house standing stark and spare at the end of a long lane winding back in time.

Intuitively she knew, as mothers often do, that long winter nights are less frightening if children are sent to bed with something besides a mournful wind blowing through their imaginations.

So she read to us as we crowded up close to the old black heating stove that turned back the chill. And when we went to bed, the demons of the dark had to compete with knights on snow-white chargers.

As I lay there the other night, with the moonlight seeping like golden mist through the open bedroom window, I remembered the stack of Ripley's "Believe It or Nots" that she had clipped daily from the newspaper because she thought we would enjoy looking at them some wintry night when we had nothing to do.

But we never got that chance because I burned them all. I don't remember why. I was mad about something, and I wiped them out in a senseless act of revenge.

Mother didn't say anything, but I remember the hurt in her eyes. Worse than that was her lack of comprehension. She couldn't understand revenge. It was alien to her nature.

She forgave me, just as she forgave me a thousand other times. And I'm amazed now that love could overcome so many hurts that cut so deep. Mother proved to me that love possesses healing powers beyond all understanding.

By modern standards hers would have been a life of drudgery and desolation. Wives who lived on farms worked hard, without the conveniences that gleam in homes today.

Sometimes, I know, her existence must have looked bleak and barren. But she had a gift that lifted her above despair. She was endowed with the belief that life is a wonder, a miracle.

The perfectly developed hand of a newborn infant, she once told me, was a sight that inspired her awe and reverence. Her mind remained fresh because it refused to take things for granted.

Recently, while looking through some pictures in her bedroom, I discovered a scrapbook that she had been adding to for more than 50 years. It is filled with clippings from newspapers and magazines.

They were inspirational, but not in a strictly religious sense. They dwelt upon the beauty that surrounds us. As they called attention to the near at hand, they spoke in muted voices of the far beyond.

She had never said anything about the scrapbook, not that I remember. But I'm not surprised. The quiet way was her way.

As I slowly turned the yellowed pages, I was reminded of a flower coming into bloom, one petal at a time.

I was out of bed by then, I was standing by the window, and all the world shimmered in a moonlit bath of beauty. I hope Mother saw it. And I hope that I saw what she would have seen. No mother can contribute more than that.

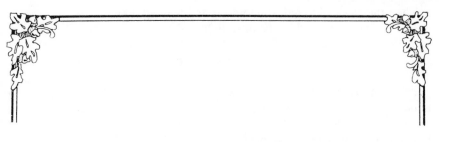

Granddad's Endless Furrow

When spring rolled around, Granddad got the urge to "commence plowing."

At the same time, the horses commenced to get that forlorn look because they knew they were in for a long siege.

He plowed with three horses hooked to a single-bottom riding plow. The wheel on the right side ran in the furrow, which was usually about six inches deep.

According to the manufacturer, it could be adjusted so the plow would ride level. But Granddad's didn't adjust that way. It always "rode a little whopperjawed," according to him.

He didn't have to tell the horses what to do after they got in the field. They knew his mind as well as he did. Together they had come down that long avenue that years of repetition had worn smooth with familiarity.

Granddad reminded me of a gnome hunched up on the seat of the plow with his hat pulled down over his ears and the reins hanging loose in his hands. With the patience of Job he sat there, hour after hour, year after year.

He was a man who lived in harmony with the land. He understood its rhythms. He treated it with patience and understanding. More than anything else he respected it.

Watching a long, black furrow unroll was a pleasure he never tired of. It was an umbilical cord that connected him directly to the land.

In Biblical times, nations were urged to pound their swords into plowshares. If Granddad had been in charge they would have. I'm not sure peace would have reigned, but I've never heard of anyone being run through with a plow.

Plowing remained his primary recreation, but he began spending less time in the fields as the years caught up with him. Some days he came in at four in the afternoon.

"Horses got tired," he'd say as he climbed off the plow and slapped old Ned on the rump. "Ain't as young as they used to be."

Then the seasons began running off and leaving him.

One spring he plowed his favorite field and harrowed it. But he didn't get it planted, and it didn't bother him a bit. As he dug a big philosophical chew of "terbaccer" out of his sack, he said: "I don't reckon it'll hurt the land to rest a year."

I thought he was slipping, but I was mistaken. He had been around long enough to realize that an unplanted crop is the one that causes the least amount of trouble. He had beaten the system. He'd enjoyed the pleasure of plowing without reaping the problems.

I like to plow almost as much as Granddad did, and last week I plowed our garden spot. And when I got to thinking about all the work it's going to take, I decided to follow Granddad's example and give it a good rest.

I'll disc it a couple of times to smooth it out, and by next spring it should be in great shape to plow again.

Future Rushes Into The Past

It came rushing out of my memory recently, with a halo of romance and adventure hovering over its shiny back.

As I watched, it came rushing down the tracks. I heard again its rumble, and the long, throaty wail of its whistle as it approached the crossing where we stood.

We were students from a small country school in Nebraska where all 12 grades were taught in two large rooms. We had walked a mile to be there when the train went by.

It wasn't just any train. It was one of the first streamlined locomotives to travel the rails of the Union Pacific. The year was 1934 -- or '35. It was the future we had come to see.

As it approached, the sleek, flowing lines of the tawny cocoon that covered the engine made me think of a rocket. It reminded me of something out of Buck Rogers. It was tomorrow making its debut.

The country was flat, and the tracks on both sides of the crossing were straight for miles. Normally trains flashed by the crossing as the ghost of a dying whistle faded away.

But it was a clear, warm day -- I believe it was early spring -- and the engineer had seen us from far down the track. As he eased up on the throttle, the engine began slowing down so we could see it better as it rolled on by.

He gave us a couple of friendly toots of the whistle as he waved. Then he shoved the throttle ahead, and we heard the big engine surge. As the last car whipped by, it was gaining speed.

It reminded me, that locomotive did, of a mighty beast, wild of whistle and fast of foot. As we walked slowly back down the graveled road to school, I hurtled with it through my imagination.

It was westward bound, and at the rim of the prairie I could see the great mountains it would cross: the snow-capped Rockies -- sheer rock walls and jagged buttes and fingers of twisted stone clawing at the sky.

Ahead I could see the tracks wrapping a steely coil around a steep mountain flank, banding it with the route the engine would ascend with a mighty rush and roar.

Then the mountains began running out, and the engine came coasting down the western slope, breathing easier as it glided smoothly into a bone-dry desert where sagebrush fretted in a restless wind, and rattlesnakes stretched in slow systolic curves.

It rolled on into the West, and I saw, far off and hazy, the smooth blue blanket of the Pacific. I saw people lying on white sandy beaches. And I watched swimmers with blowing hair run into the slow lift of lazy waves that uncurled upon the shore.

In that mile walk back to school, I traveled 10,000 miles. It was a journey I've never forgotten. It's still fresh. The rails still clack cleanly beneath the wheels, and the sound is the sound of magic.

Railroads were king then. Passengers were pampered, and delays were few and far between. When conductors checked their watches and shouted, "All aboard," big wheels began to roll. Time was a treasure not to be wasted.

I thought of that with a sense of loss when I heard recently that Amtrak may be headed for the scrap pile. It was ironic, I thought, that we had been lured to that crossing to see a future that has already become obsolete.

Years ago, with the lonely cry of a grieving whistle, that engine rolled to a stop. It came to rest on a deserted siding, stiffly a-bristle with the stalks of last year's dying weeds. It may not be alone much longer.

Another technological journey may be coming to an end. The last call for tickets may have already sounded. Amtrak trains may soon take their place beside that streamliner we waited to see on a distant country crossing 50 years ago.

An Amazing Menagerie

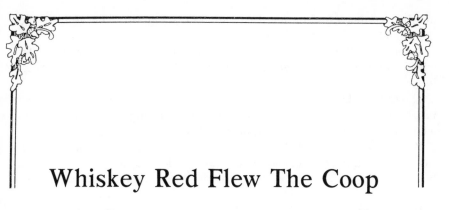

Whiskey Red Flew The Coop

Slim raised fighting roosters. He had them staked out all over the side of a long sloping hill, next to small, individual A-frame shelters.

They produced quite a melody on an early summer morning. And their red feathers glistened in the sun as they preened and paraded at the end of their tethers.

It is legal to raise fighting cocks in Oregon, but it is illegal to fight them. However, if laws are to be broken, as some contend, I suppose that one has been badly bent.

But not by Slim. Not to hear him tell it. He said he raised fighting chickens to sell, and that was all. He did quite a foreign business. Hundreds of his proud, glossy-feathered roosters went to the Philippines.

I know they did because he showed me a pile of orders he had received. His roosters brought a premium, he said, because they were full of fight. They looked it. Their eyes were bright and hard and mean.

One day I stopped to see him about some calves he wanted to sell. While we were wandering around the hillside looking at his roosters, he picked out a couple of young ones whose fighting spirit he wanted to check.

In the end of a long shed where he kept the hens that laid the eggs that produced the roosters, there was a small wire enclosure. When he tossed the roosters into it, they took one long, malevolent look at each other before getting acquainted in a most violent way.

They literally exploded. They were so fast I couldn't tell what was happening to whom. After the first flurry Slim moved in to break them up. While he was holding the rooster he had grabbed, the other one continued to attack.

As he slipped through the gate with the rooster under his arm, Slim decided it would do okay someday in some foreign fighting pit. "Good blood," he said, with a satisfied nod. "He'll do good in the Philippines."

When he said that I thought of my brother Buggs, who was a soldier in the Philippines when World War II ended. With the fighting over, soldiers

29

didn't have much to do while they waited for the government to discharge them, and time began to drag.

To occupy himself, a friend of his decided to pick up some extra money with fighting roosters. When he thought he had found a good one, he bought it.

The fellow who sold him claimed Whiskey Red was the finest rooster that had ever entered a pit. Put spurs on him, he told Buggs' buddy, and he'll whip an elephant. Or a water buffalo, at least.

Buggs said his buddy babied Whiskey Red along. He gave him the best of care. He was treated like money in the bank, which he was certainly going to be. When he was in top condition, his friend decided the time to fight had come.

He was a persuasive talker, said Buggs, and he convinced nearly everyone in the outfit that Whiskey Red was going to be the supreme rooster in all the Philippine Islands.

"You want to go home rich," he told them, "just lay your money on Whiskey Red."

A lot of them did. Buggs was among them. Expectations were running high, and suspense filled the air as his buddy moved into the pit for Whiskey Red's much publicized debut. When the signal was given the roosters were released.

There was a moment of hesitation as the roosters eyed each other, said Buggs. Then Whiskey Red flared up and all those who had bet on him stood in open-mouthed amazement as they watched him fly out of the pit and disappear.

Late that night, Buggs said his buddy came lurching drunkenly through camp. He was looking for Whiskey Red. "He'll make a pot of stew if I ever find him," he mumbled as he stumbled off.

I like that. I like it better than the sight of Slim's roosters staked out all over a sloping hillside. I'm not sure why. Maybe it's because the tables were turned, and the rooster that created a stew among the bettors left them with an empty pot.

Momma Kitty's Cruel Game

With binoculars I watch Momma Kitty glide like a sleek, grey phantom across the field. She looms large, wide-eyed and alert.

She's hunting. She doesn't have to. Her dish on the back porch is full of her favorite food. I can only guess at her reason for slinking across a hayfield in a hot midday sun.

Some say it's an instinct so deeply embedded in Momma Kitty's brain it cannot be ignored. Even if she were surrounded by mountains of Crave, they say, she would remain a predator.

Now she's flattened out on her belly. She's still as a graceful carving, one small package of deadliness poised for plunder. It's still, as though time itself is holding its breath.

So slowly it's almost imperceptible, she lifts one front foot and moves it forward, tentatively, the way a chess player does when the game is coming to an end.

The tip of her tail flicks, but there's no other movement for a full minute. Then she takes another agonizingly slow step forward. She's time arrested -- time stopped.

I cannot see with the binoculars what she sees. But I feel my hands and arms grow tense because there's something about death and violence that intrigues the human mind.

Perhaps it shouldn't: it's so elemental, such a fact of life. Maybe our fascination has increased as we have tried to rise above it. Maybe we've drawn closer as we've tried to draw away.

Like a coiled spring Mama Kitty explodes into the air. Her back is bowed and her head is down. She hangs there for a moment in the sun like a half-done question mark.

Then she falls, and there is no question any more. í can imagine the wild terror of the field mouse the instant it sensed danger. Perhaps her soundless shadow was the signal it saw too late.

With it trapped between her paws, Momma Kitty lies there as she looks around. Then, with a practiced dip of her head, she picks it up and starts for the house.

She comes easily down through the field. She flows smoothly like deep water, and I know where she is headed. We've been through this before.

Once or twice she stops to rest her jaws, I suppose, while she holds the mouse with an unrelenting paw. Then she comes in, daintily picking her way through the stiff brown stubble.

When she reaches the yard she stops again and looks toward the house. When she sees me on the deck, she seems relieved. She seems to wait a moment longer with the mouse trapped beneath her paw so I can appreciate the thing she's done.

I move over to the edge so she won't bring the mouse up on the deck, which she'll do if she doesn't think I'm paying her enough attention.

For a while she plays with the mouse on the grass. She sits down and watches it scurry away. Then in one long leap she captures it, and looks around to see if I have noticed.

I assume Mother Nature knows what she's about. She seems to. Every time we humans upset the balance she tries to maintain we seem to pay. But I've never understood the meaning of this cruel game that Momma Kitty plays.

To the victor goes the spoils: that's what it appears to emphasize. And when victors tire of the game, they end it just as Momma Kitty will.

When she looks up at me, she meows. She's very vain about her predatory prowess. As I watch her I think of victorious armies on parade -- and cemeteries -- and miles of small white crosses.

A Nest For Frustration

Cattle, horses, sheep and hogs will usually be where they shouldn't be -- if given half a chance.

But they're exemplary models of behavior compared to chickens. As he shooed a bunch of hens off a sack of feed they had pecked a big hole into, an old man once said to me, "God never breathed life into nothing as no-account."

As he cleaned up the mess they had made, he said the Almighty must have been "feeling poorly" the morning He put feathers on whatever it was He started out with to make chickens. Then he blasted Noah for letting them on the Ark.

"Too bad the whole passel didn't sink," he mumbled disgustedly, as he rummaged around in the dim light of the barn for a needle and thread to mend the sack.

If you've had much to do with chickens, you will be quick to second everything the old man said. If you're not quick to second what he said, you were acquainted with a different breed of chickens than it was my good fortune to meet.

I don't suppose you could expect too much from them -- along intellectual lines, at least. They don't have much room for a lot of learning. With their brains all squinched up that way I'm amazed they know as much as they do. What amazes me even more is the fact that most everything they know would make life more pleasant if they didn't know it.

For instance:

How do they know where the choicest flowers are planted? They must have an instinctive yen for beauty before it blooms because they can scratch up a prize row of petunias quicker than a charge card bill comes due.

And that's just for openers. Where they really shine is in a freshly planted garden. Since they've got eyes on both sides of their heads they can see right and left at the same time, which gives them a distinct advantage.

An old hen with a little experience can rip up two rows of radishes at once without so much as turning her head. There's no doubt about it, chickens were designed for double-barrel destruction.

If they can't crawl through a fence -- or wriggle under it -- or find a crack around the gate to sneak through -- they'll fly over it to get at something you're trying to keep them out of.

For that reason we never penned ours up. As long as they were on their own, they were expected to fend for themselves. Naturally, that saved feed and the time it would have taken to clean a hen house out.

But there was something wrong with that system. The equation seemed weighted in their favor. I could have cleaned a hen house out in half the time I spent hunting the eggs our hens laid.

I've looked high and low for nests they advertised with an arrogant cackle after they had laid an egg in some obscure corner of the barn. I've waded through thickets of cobwebs for those I never found. Even when I did, I was usually out of luck.

I don't know how they did it, but those hens could hide a nest I could never find until it had been discovered by a stray dog looking for a fresh omelette -- or a raccoon -- or a skunk.

What impudence those old hens had. They strutted around with the mien of queens. Their beady-little-glittery eyes were contemptuous of anything that resembled a human being. They made me feel guilty as a shoplifter every time I accidentally stumbled upon an egg they would occasionally let me find.

How things have changed. Recently, I was in one of those modern egg factories, where hens are stuffed into cages so small they can hardly move. What a dispirited bunch they were as they squatted in those tight, wiry confines.

They didn't act like they were remotely related to the arrogant species that irreverently littered our barn with droppings. They were more easily managed, that was for sure, but all the flash and fire was gone. They had no spark left.

Lack of freedom had taken the crackle out of their cackle. Lack of freedom will do it every time.

Cattle Have The Strangest Appetites

Sam and his hired man were filling a silo with ensilage. The silo was in the corral next to the barn, and the cows wre milling around waiting to be milked. Then a bolt sheared off in the chopper, and half of it had to be drilled out because it rusted tight in the hole. As Sam's boy strung out the electric cord for the drill, he had to boot the cows out of the way.

It didn't take long to replace the bolt, and within 30 minutes they were through chopping ensilage and Sam crawled up on the tractor and eased it ahead to loosen the belt that drove the chopper. As he rolled up the belt, he told his boy to finish cleaning up around the chopper so he and the hired man could start milking.

"And don't forget to roll up the electric cord," he said.

Tim nodded. He was 11. He was hot and sweaty. Cleaning up around ensilage choppers, and rolling up electric cords were way down on the list of things he wanted to do. Thoughts of the swimming hole down at the river were splashing through his mind as he slouched across the corral.

They must have swamped his mind because he forgot to roll up the cord and the next morning one of his dad's top Holstein cows lay deader than a doornail in the corral. She had tried to eat the electric cord and Sam figured it had electrocuted her after she had "wallered" the insulation off.

Tim didn't get the hide wallered off his rear end but he knew it was getting thin by the time his dad got through with him. I'm sure he got more of a charge out of a pair of willow switches than that cow had gotten out of all the current in the cord.

That proves one thing: Cattle have strange ways of appeasing even stranger appetites. That point was dramatically demonstrated recently by a 400-pound steer we owned. He drank half a five-gallon can full of old, thick-black, dirty crankcase oil. I don't know if it satisfied the compulsive craving that had seized him, but it certainly solved his problems -- permanently. When we refer to him now it's in the past tense.

35

That was bad enough, but his untimely demise created quite another problem. He had been calved late last year and his mother was still giving too much milk to dry up. After I had milked her for a couple of days, I decided to graft another calf on her. It was such a good idea I wondered why I hadn't thought of it before.

No one in the neighborhood had a calf for sale, so I wound up making an 80-mile round trip to an auction. So many calves had to be sold before I got the one I wanted, there wasn't much daylight left by the time I got home. And the old cow didn't greet him with anything that resembled motherly love and affection.

She took one nervous little sniff of him, slipped her nose under his belly and flipped him half the length of the barn. She wasn't about to take on a baby that wasn't maternally hers.

For the one she'd lost she continued to grieve. For three straight days she bawled and bawled and wouldn't eat. And the little calf bawled and bawled because she wouldn't give him any milk, even though I snubbed her up tight so he could suck to his heart's content.

Finally I gave up. I turned the cow out. As she bawled her way to the end of the pasture in search of her calf, I headed for the feed store and a $10 sack of milk replacer. Since then I've become mother to a little bull calf that would much rather be mothered by a cow. If I had my druthers, he would get his wish.

His foster mother that wouldn't be, is doing fine. When her period of mourning ended, she began eating grass with great green gusto. Her udder swelled up tight and now she has to be milked again. So I catch her whener swelled up tight and now she has to be milked again. So I catch her whenever she allows herself to be caught and we fight to see who gets her milk.

Sometimes they'll just about drive you to drink anything -- short of old crankcase oil.

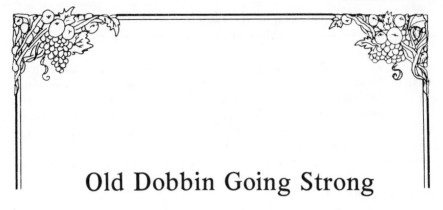

Old Dobbin Going Strong

I thought draft horses were a thing of the past. When tractors took over I thought they would go the way of the dodo bird. By now I expected them to be extinct.

I didn't realize how mistaken I was until last June. At an auction sponsored by the Small Farmers Journal in Eugene we sold enough horse drawn equipment to outfit a wagon train.

It came from everywhere: from all over the Northwest and Missouri and Utah -- and hundreds of nooks and crannies where it had been stored for years. And people came from miles around to buy old wagons, mowing machines, plows and harrows, hay rakes, corn planters and cultivators.

I thought I had seen nearly every piece of horse drawn equipment that had been designed, but again I was mistaken. From out of the past came lots of surprises.

Take the left-handed plow, for instance. Instead of turning soil to the right as most plows do, it turned it to the left. I'm not sure why, unless the designer forgot which way the horses were headed when he bolted it together.

I thought by now most of the old harnesses had rotted away, except for a few sets preserved for posterity. How wrong I was.

I don't know how many sets were sold, nor how many miscellaneous straps and buckles and bridles were auctioned off, but there was enough to harness Budweiser commercials for the next 50 years.

And horse collars -- of all shapes and sizes -- were in abundance. Forty were brand new. They had come from the Midwest. Some sold for more than $100 each.

Several buggies were there, but one stands out in my mind. It was an old enclosed Amish buggy from Missouri. It was black and square, with a windshield that could be raised and lowered and curtains for windows in the doors.

It was without adornment of any kind. It had been designed to serve without pretense, humbly, without show. If it reflected one quality above all others it was simple honesty.

A sleigh was a real eye-catcher. It was highly varnished, fancy and ornate. It had two plush seats upholstered in velvety green. It looked like something any horse would have been proud to pull.

As interesting as the equipment assembled there were the people who had congregated for the auction. They had come from all walks of life because love of horses afflicts people of every age.

Lots of oldtimers had come to take one more look at the handles, the rusty levers, and the long black reins that had put calluses on their hands when horses were the only way to go.

Some were retired and lived in town. A few still had farms and horses they worked because that was their life. They had big knobby hands, and ruddy faces. They watched with calm, quiet eyes.

One fellow had flown in from New Mexico. He was a businessman, who raised draft horses as a hobby. He was looking for someone with a truck. If he bought something he wanted to get it hauled.

A couple from California had driven down from Portland where they were visiting relatives to attend the sale. They bought nearly all the old iron equipment seats that were offered.

They were going to use them on picnic tables they were building for a place they owned in the mountains. They paid from $15 to $20 apiece for them. They were happy to find them.

But not much of the equipment was bought for novel uses or ornamental purposes. Most of it was sold to horse farmers who are putting it to work on farms where old Dobbin is making a comeback.

He is plodding out of the past to recapture the present. And those who rely on him say old Dobbin's future is assured.

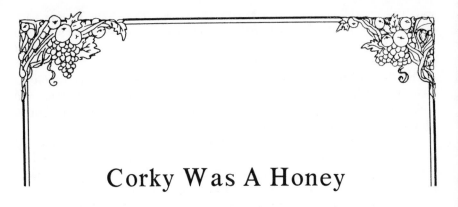

Corky Was A Honey

Corky was a pet raccoon that will live in my memory as long as I have one. I can still feel the soft, restless, caressing curiosity of his fingers as they slipped shyly into my shirt pocket to search for anything that was there. And I can still see the crafty, daring and defiant look on his face the day we caught him in the cupboard dipping honey out of a jar with both hands.

He knew he was going to get it, but he was a bold spirit, a fearless little lawbreaker who refused to give an inch. He growled to let us know he didn't appreciate an interruption. We were surprised to find him there. We didn't think he could get in the house.

He was a smart little thief. One day when he didn't think we were around, we watched him climb the screen door. He hung on with one hand when he got to the top and pushed against the casing with the other to force the door open. After he had swung around the edge, he let himself down on the inside. He had clear sailing then. Mother left the kitchen door open during the summer to keep the house cool.

After he had crawled upon a chair, we watched him climb upon the kitchen table. From there it was a short jump to the counter below the cupboard, where we had caught him sticky-fingered.

Shiny things attracted him. If they weren't shiny when he found them, he did his best to polish them with his quick black fingers. If there was any around, he would dip them in water to bring out their brightest lustre.

Corky became a member of our household long before most rural areas had been electrified, and the only electricity we had was supplied by what my folks called the "old Delco plant." It was a gasoline engine hooked to a generator that was connected to a series of batteries. When it worked, it worked fine. When it didn't, it usually had to be overhauled.

On one occasion, a part deep inside the engine went on the blink and it had to be ordered. While he was waiting for it, Dad left the nuts and bolts on the floor, along with an assortment of greasy parts. When the gear, or

39

sprocket, or whatever it was arrived, Dad started to put the engine back together, but he couldn't. All the nuts and bolts were gone. It took some doing, but my brother and sister and I finally convinced him we hadn't carted them off to use as slingshot shells.

Then he noticed Corky, who was listening with a smug little smirk on his face. Dad studied him for a moment, then walked over to the work bench and picked up a bolt. As he dropped it on the floor, he motioned for us to follow. Through a crack in the door, we watched from an adjoining room.

As soon as he thought he was alone, Corky snatched up the bolt and disappeared behind some boxes stacked up next to the wall. There we found the rest of the nuts and bolts, shining like silver dollars. Fixing that Delco plant was not a job Dad enjoyed, and those missing bolts hadn't improved his disposition. We figured Corky was going to get it, and we held our breath. When Dad laughed, we were relieved.

Then, one morning in early spring, Corky was gone. I guess he had heard the call of the wild and it was too strong to resist. He came back once to visit. Before he left, he laid waste to a bunch of baby chickens Mother was raising. We never saw him again. He probably decided that for once he had gone too far. And he was right. If he had returned, he would have been in deep trouble.

Corky left, but he isn't gone. He's an image in my mind that's never faded. Wherever he went, I hope he found cupboards with no doors and honey brimming from a dozen jars.

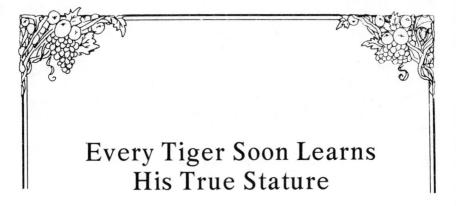

Every Tiger Soon Learns His True Stature

I shouldn't have named him Tiger. He sure doesn't look like one. Except for white feet and a small white triangle under his nose he is black.

He looks more like a Halloween cat than anything else. But I called him Tiger because it could be shortened to Tig, which is easy to say.

When I got him, Tig was a tiny kitten. He was a gift from Jackie, our daughter-in-law. He came from a litter that was born in a field next to her house.

The kittens were wild as March hares, and it took Jackie a long time to convince Tig that she was a friend. When he found out how well she fed, he wasn't at all reluctant about giving up his wild and woolly ways.

At first I let him roam around the house. He did fine until he realized who he was. Then his personality changed. He immediately took a dislike to the couch and tried to tear it apart the way a ferocious tiger should.

After the couch had been subdued, he turned on an overstuffed chair. By the time he had it cowering raggedly in the corner, he had scratched up the piano, too. Then he proceeded to claw the stuffing out of a dining room chair.

He was a destructive streak that moved with the speed of light. Before you could say, "Here he comes," he had. And everything in his wake was tattered and torn.

He didn't like it when I moved him outside, but he quickly adapted. And he has thrived in the great outdoors. He may not look like a Tiger but he's going to be as big as one if he keeps growing.

When he found that he was on his own, he began prowling the fields. Then he started hunting and anything that moved became fair game.

First, he declared war on the leaves that skittered across the yard. By now they must hate the wind that catches Tig's attention when it stirs them up.

The bigger he got the more arrogant he became. In his big green eyes a cold light began to gleam. He was fast embracing the idea that he was superior to everyone -- and everything.

During the summer I used a bunch of wooden blocks to prop up a building that I put a foundation under. After I was through I tossed them into a pile.

When I went to move them a month later, Tig was there. In fact, he was everywhere. If he wasn't under foot, he was on top of the block I was about to pick up. He seemed to know that in there somewhere he would find a treat.

Great hunters have an instinct for such things, I guess, and for Tig it paid off. Under the last block was a field mouse that had strayed too far from its hole. The rodent must have thought it was a goner when Tig came down upon it, and so did I.

But the Great Hunter wanted to enjoy his conquest by letting the mouse loose so he could pounce upon it as it tried to escape. Each time he let it stray a little farther before he made his move.

As the game went on, the tip of Tig's tail began to flick with boredom. Obviously, he was much impressed by his prowess. As he was congratulating himself he let the mouse stray too far and it got away.

Tig couldn't believe it. He looked and looked where he had seen it last. Then he expanded his search 100 feet in every direction, but to no avail. The mouse was gone.

Finally, he gave up. But he didn't give up hope. With imploring eyes and a plaintive yowl he asked me for help. When I turned him down, he left. I noticed a decided droop in his tail as he departed.

I feel guilty for the funk he's in. When I named him Tiger I'm sure I gave him an inflated sense of his own worth. And nothing hurts worse than becoming what you are after thinking you were so much more.

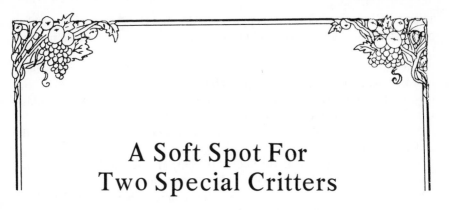

A Soft Spot For
Two Special Critters

Cattle are a commodity. In time, those who raise them begin viewing them as so many dollars, nothing more. When milk cows no longer produce, or butcher cattle reach the right weight and condition, they go to market. There's not much sentiment involved. The cattle industry is business, big business.

Even so, every once in a while a critter will catch your eye. By its spirit, a cow or calf will linger on in the memory after all others have been forgotten. For two that I saw while I was in the auction business, I have a soft spot in my heart.

One was a little, wooly, black white-faced calf that had lost its mother. I don't know what happened to her. Maybe she died, or had been sold because it's not uncommon to split cows and calves if it looks like they will bring more when sold separately.

Anyway, one morning there he was in the corral, one of a load of cattle that we had bought. Unlike most calves of that age, he didn't stand around bawling. He was an independent, hard-headed little dogie, and he went right to work sizing up the situation. He was smart, and it didn't take him long to learn the ropes. By his wits he lived. He would have made a good con man.

Because old cows don't like to take on boarders, he soon found that he couldn't move in on another calf's meal ticket. So he would wait until a calf was sucking, and the old mother cow was daydreaming about whatever it is old mother cows dream about, then he would ease in and find a spare faucet. Usually, it was a short meal at most, because the cow would wise up in a minute or two and send him not too gently on his way. By that method he survived.

We began calling him Tuffy. And, for some reason, whenever we rounded up cattle to sell, Tuffy always found the gate open to him.

He was an indomitable little devil, tough and defiant. I can still see him making his stand when crowded. Coolly, he would back off, but only so far.

Then he would toss his head a couple of times, and the fight was on. He had guts, which is an admirable quality, regardless of the size or shape it comes in.

The other one I will probably never forget was a soft-eyed little brindle cow that had been bred too young. When the time came, she just couldn't give birth. There was too much calf, and not enough of her. After working with her for hours without success, we called the vet.

"It's no use," he said after taking a look at her, "we'll have to take the calf to save her."

With her stretched out on the floor of the barn, he began. By then, she had suffered so long I don't think she cared. It had been an ordeal, and when the incision was made we took the calf through a hole in her side. It was dead.

"But I think we can save her," Doc said, as he sorted around for a needle to close the incision.

She couldn't get up that night, so I bedded her pen with fresh straw and carried water and feed to her. When she finally made it to her feet, she was still weak and uncertain. For about a week we kept her penned separately and treated her like one of the family.

She made fine progress, and after a week we turned her out in the long feeding barn with the rest of the cattle. For several days she did fine. Then some cow trying to hog the feed trough hooked her in the side and ruptured the incision. This time nothing could be done for her.

She was a gentle spirit. She harmed no one. After all the suffering she had been through, I'm convinced that she was entitled to better than she got. Sometimes it seems that there just ain't no justice.

Of Heifers And New Born Calves

Once we had a heifer who appeared well on her way to becoming an average, easy-going, good-natured cow. She wasn't spooky. She wasn't wild. She was as easy to handle as most range cattle are.

Then she had a calf -- her first one. She didn't have an easy time of it. And when she took a look at her new baby, she let out more of a bleat than a bawl and took off. She would have nothing to do with that calf. One look was enough.

Apparently, it had caused her enough trouble and she wanted no more of it. We had to milk her by hand, and feed the calf from a bucket. Anyone who has ever tried to milk a range cow will tell you that riding a bucking bronco is less trouble.

That is rare. But rarer still was the heifer we had that tried to kill her first born calf. She was a psycho, that's all there was to it.

She was a full-blooded Shorthorn. She was eligible for registration, but we never registered her. It was just as well. Annie Laurie would have blemished the record of every self respecting Shorthorn in the association.

When she was about 10 months old, she was a beauty. She was big for her age, and as affectionate as a dog. But one day in the pasture she came charging playfully up to me as she usually did. Then suddenly she stopped. A strange, surprised look slipped into her eyes, and she began backing up as though she had seen something she didn't understand. Then her legs stiffened, and she toppled over. Her eyes rolled back and she began trembling. She began to shake convulsively. I thought she was dying. But she wasn't.

A veterinarian told me she lacked phosphorous. That, he said, was the reason she chewed on boards, bones, or anything else she could get ahold of. And her tastes for such things bizarre did seem to abate after we began mixing phosphorous with her feed.

She was bred to a Charolais bull. When she was due, we put her in the barn. We wanted her where we could assist if we were needed, because

45

Charolais calves are usually large of bone and big of head. Early every morning I checked her. But she was in no rush. She was going to give birth at her convenience.

Then one morning before I had gone to the barn to see how she was doing, I heard her bawling. But she didn't really sound like a cow. There was something angry and frightened in the sounds she was making. I started running but I knew before I got there what I would find. I was mistaken.

She wasn't having calving trouble. She had already had the calf, and was doing her level best to kill it. The only thing that saved it was the gutter that ran down the center of the barn. She had shoved the calf into that, and it was too low for her to get at with her horns. Not until I got a club could I drive her back. And she was still making that strange, angry frightened sound.

We penned them separately, and milked her to feed the calf. But it was strangely pathetic the way she acted. She sensed that the calf was hers, but in some mysterious way it frightened her. She seemed to be in a real dilemma. In time she owned Benny, but it took a week or so before she would allow him to suck -- and then only if we had her tied and were standing there to keep her from kicking his head off.

Animals don't often do things like that. They take care of their young. Annie Laurie was an exception. She was a disappointment. She acted too much like some human beings to suit me.

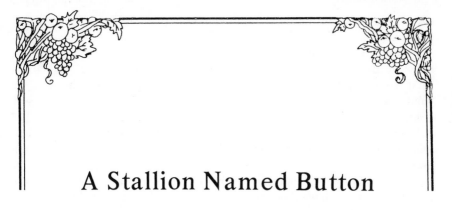

A Stallion Named Button

I know of no animal that has the flair, the grace, the pride and intensity of a stallion. Of all living things, they seem the most vital, the most alive. Life flashes in their eyes. They know they are supreme. Theirs is a beautiful arrogance.

Breeding and size has nothing to do with it. Each of them is a conquering spirit, willful and headstrong. Button was no exception though he only weighed 250 pounds.

He belonged to my brother, Buggs, who had bought him because he wanted to raise colts from the two Shetland mares he owned. They were dandies.

They each had a harness with all the trappings, and when he hooked them to the small white wagon with four red wheels, they looked like miniature draft horses pulling a toy. They attracted a lot of attention. But they weren't in the same league with Button.

Where the mares were brown and white, he was black and white. They outweighed him by 100 pounds apiece, but Buttons didn't know he was small. In his opinion, he was as big as the biggest horse that walked. He looked like a champion when he came dancing out of his pen with his nostrils flared and his eyes rolling. With his neck arched, and his head held high, he let everyone know that he was a force to be reckoned with. He was a little devil, and a delight to watch.

But one day his amorousness nearly undid him. As soon as he discovered that someone had forgotten to latch the gate of his pen, he headed for an old saddle horse mare in the pasture. She wasn't one bit impressed by all his squealing and prancing and dancing. When she'd had enough of his nonsense, she whirled and blasted him with both hind feet.

She caught him just right and snapped his right rear leg halfway between his hoof and knee. That night we found him hobbling around with his broken leg swinging limp as an old dishrag. Normally a horse in that condition is put

47

out of his misery, but Buggs couldn't stand the thought of that. So he called the vet.

Because horses don't consume as much protein as meat-eating animals, Doc said the chances of the bone knitting were pretty slim.

At our insistence, he finally agreed to give a try. But first, he said, we would have to rig a sling to keep Button off his feet while it healed -- if it was going to.

We rigged the sling, and tried to hold Button still as Doc splinted the leg, and put on the cast. When he finished, he said: "Now all we can do is wait and see."

Button didn't enjoy his confinement. He knickered and fretted, but we kept him there until we thought his leg was solid enough to hold him. Even under such crippling conditions, he maintained that indomitable pride which kept the fire flashing in his eyes.

At that time, we were in the auction business and Doc came every week to inspect and test cattle that were to be sold. Each week he checked to see how Button was doing. After inspecting him one day, he decided to give him one more week before he removed the cast. But the next week, he delayed another week.

"I'm afraid to take it off," he said, "I don't know what we'll find."

But the day came when he could delay no longer, and we all gathered around to witness the results. Slowly, he cut away the cast. Button's leg was slightly bowed, but it had healed. Doc took a deep breath as he glanced up.

"We're lucky," he said. "It was a long shot."

A bowed leg didn't bother Button a bit. He was like some people. He had so much going for him you didn't notice the blemishes.

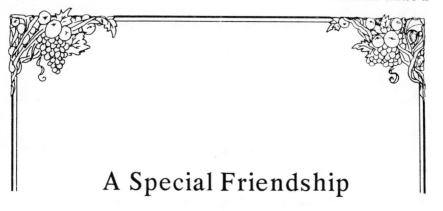

A Special Friendship

Most animals are social creatures. They like company. If one of their own is not around, they will often become friends with animals of another species. Nearly everyone is familiar with cats and dogs that become friends. In some rare instances, even dogs and rabbits become friends. There are all sorts of combinations.

One of the strangest was the friendship that existed between a black bear cub and an old collie dog. The cub had been captured by some loggers when very small, and the fellow who kept him turned him loose with the dog. They had no trouble at all, except when the lazy old collie would nip the cub for pestering him when he was trying to sleep. I don't know how they would have gotten along later, because the fellow donated the bear to a zoo before he was half grown.

Animals apparently come together out of some deep need for companionship. Friendships forged out of loneliness are often long and enduring. And no animal ever demonstrated the meaning of friendship more persistently than did old Jake.

He was a big, curly black and white shepherd dog we once owned. He was a noble animal even though he was of mixed ancestry. He had a large square head and the most attentive, intelligent eyes you've ever seen. He was friendly, kind and generous. I never knew of him to bite -- or even growl when we aggravated him, which kids have a tendency to do.

He was an outside dog. He was never allowed in the house. That was the rule. He was going to be a working dog, and Dad didn't want him spoiled. Although he would have been considered a mutt by most dog breeders, he was a natural born heeler, which was a trait bestowed upon him by one of his ancestors because heeling is an inherited characteristic. Not many dogs come with it.

He was considered one of the best stock dogs in the country. Once after he had helped load a bull Dad had sold, the buyer offered to add $150 to the

49

check if he could take Jake along. That was a lot of money then, but Dad refused.

As most dogs have, Jake had a built-in timer. Each afternoon he would amble off to the pasture and bring the cows in for milking. He didn't have to be told. It was his job and he did it at the same time every day.

It was uncanny, but he knew how many cows there were. He never missed one, even though they burrowed deep into the brush to elude him. When he brought them up, he brought them all. Until we turned out four small heifers that had been penned in the barn during the winter. When they joined the herd, things changed.

Jake's routine didn't. He still went to the pasture for the cattle each afternoon. He still brought up all the cattle -- unless one of those heifers didn't want to come. From Jake they received preferential treatment. He absolutely wouldn't drive them.

He would go back down into the pasture when Dad ordered him to bring them up, but it was a ploy. He wouldn't touch them. When finally we would give up and go after them, he would be there. Even though he knew he was going to get his ears pulled, he would not run, whimper or cower. He had class. He accepted his punishment stoically, but those heifers remained untouched.

Then it dawned on us. During one of those long, cold Nebraska winters he had bedded down with them before they were big enough to turn out. They had kept each other warm during those frigid wind-whipped nights. They were his friends, and he wouldn't mistreat them. And he never did.

A Treasury of
Sights and Sounds

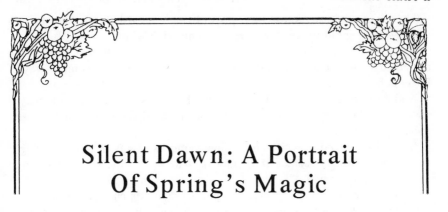

Silent Dawn: A Portrait Of Spring's Magic

In the dark of long March evenings, frogs begin talking about the spring that is on its way.

In the swales, where bulrushes grow, they announce in gravelly voices that it won't be long until the sun comes early to give each day a longer life.

And soon it does.

And a rooster raises its voice like a raising banner to greet a pearl grey hour of dawn, and a mile away it is answered by another early riser. In that stillness it lingers for a moment, so clear it should be seen.

At that special hour their voices float like sails on a sea of quiet, drifting slow in ancient rhythm before they sink back into the silence that absorbs them.

Spring is magic in the quiet of early morning, during the hush between a rooster's crow and the harsh grinding sounds of a world waking up for another day of industrial bedlam.

It is a cat coming slowly across the lawn from a long night's perilous adventure, followed by a wispy trail in the dew-drenched grass.

With the softness of a shadow, with the slow grace of a phantom dancer, it goes toward the house, the hunter returning like a pulse of pre-historic time flashed back to the beginning.

With one paw raised, it stops and lifts its head. It has heard, and now it sees the twittering bird sitting like a tiny balloon fluffed upon the branch.

They eye each other, and for an instant it slips into that fragile moment: the law of the claw, violence and quick death. For an instant the moment is in danger.

The sun is lifting a misty halo above the black and broken backs of the mountains as the cat breaks stance with a flick of its tail and steps daintily through the grass.

When spring is an early morning everything becomes more than it was in harsh daylight. A subtle change in softer light imbues it with a greater depth.

The mystery that we sense has not yet been bombarded into some forlorn corner of our mind by all that must be contended with.

Albeit short, there is time enough to watch the shadow from a tree stretch out absurdly long and lean in the sun's first rays -- Nature's comical way of introducing the new day.

And there is time to look at clover folded tight as tiny napkins the way it stays at night. And time to watch it hold a grand reopening in the early morning light.

Daffodils arrayed in white and yellow stand like flags in parade-straight rows when spring becomes that time of year again, the color guard that salutes it upon arrival.

From a pond down in the marsh a pair of mallards chatter softly to each other before they sense someone coming. Then up they come, pumping hard and fast as they bank left to become dim black dots fading into disappearance.

But the special morning moment is coming to an end. The hush is lifting and day is slipping in.

The rooster's crow does not sound in the rising sun, and the bird no longer twitters sleepily. The cat is stretched out on the porch, and somewhere on a distant flight a pair of mallards look down on strange terrain. The clover has unfolded and daffodils stand at parade rest.

On a distant hill a truck begins to strain, and someone honks a horn. The spell is broken -- day has come.

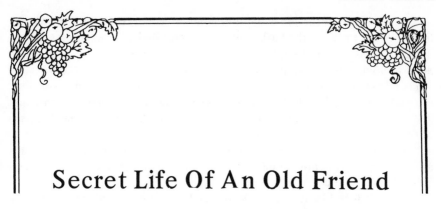

Secret Life Of An Old Friend

It resembles a shaggy wolf's ravenous head when looked at from one angle.

From another, it looks like one of those conical headdresses that women of some native tribes wear like crowns.

From the other side it appears to be a tired old woman a little on the blowsy side, wearing a skirt with a raggedy hem.

But it deceives. It's none of those. It's a quince tree that grows in our backyard. They aren't rare, but quince trees don't abound in this country. Originally, they came from central Asia.

They bear something that resembles an apple. It's about the same size, and it ripens to a light yellow. But there the resemblance ends. It's hard as a rock, and it tastes like a quince, which isn't good.

Quinces are used to flavor marmalade and jelly. Or used to be. Anyway, I don't think many people even know they exist. In today's streamlined, assembly-line society, where synthetics substitute for nearly everything, they don't really have a place.

That's the reason I decided to cut our quince tree down. It wasn't in the right place, as far as I was concerned. I couldn't even find a place where I thought it would look appropriate.

Not that I would move it, even if there had been. It's too big for one thing. And who would want to preserve anything that looked so tired and tattered.

I was ready to bring it down. Then one day I saw a pair of robins come gliding in with that anxious, worried look that parents often have. And I listened to their scolding voices as they disappeared among the leaves.

That saved it for the time being. I didn't want my conscience burdened by the thought that I had deliberately wrecked a home. And a nice cool home at that -- one that's rocked gently in every breeze.

But it was only a reprieve, of that I was determined. When the birds left, it would have to go. I had made up my mind.

As I walked by it the other day I stopped to look at its bent and twisted limbs. When I noticed the bark peeling off in patches like impetigo scabs, I decided it was a good thing I was going to get rid of it. Otherwise, it would need treatment by a chiropractor and a dermatologist.

Then I noticed something else. All but buried in the dark green leaves was the playhouse the kids had built years ago in the notch formed by the fork just above the trunk. It had been there so long -- and had become such a part of the tree - I had forgotten about it.

Now it's a jumble of grey boards, bubbly plywood separating at the seams, and rusty, bent-over nails that dodged the enthusiastic hammers the kids wielded as they made a dream come true.

It doesn't look like it, but I can remember when that playhouse was a mansion. I can recall days when it was a palace -- the finest around. And I know it's been the cockpit of an airplane, the cab of a truck, and all the exciting things that live -- that really live -- in small and fertile imaginations.

And now I notice something else. My conscience is beginning to chastise me. It won't let me forget about all the things that tree has been -- and will be if I don't cut it down. Naturally, it fights unfairly, the way a conscience does, because there is no switch that turns it off.

Slowly it has changed my attitude. And from my new perspective that tree no longer looks unsightly. The bent and twisted limbs are no longer deformed, they are just tired and worn. And I've decided the bark it's shedding is nothing more than a minor rash.

It reminds me now of the quiet dignity, the patient strength, that is acquired by those who serve so long and faithfully.

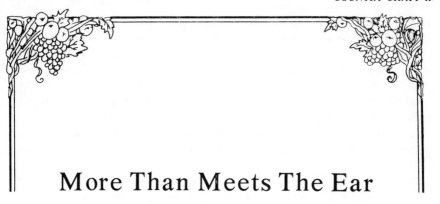

More Than Meets The Ear

Nature speaks with many voices.

I was thinking about that the other night as I lay in bed and listened to coyotes howling back and forth to each other in the deep, dark silence.

And I wondered what primordial message they were relaying across all the eons of their existence. I tried hard to catch their inflections, to detect a subtle shift of intonation.

I couldn't. But, I thought, that doesn't mean it isn't there. A sound so shrill we can't hear it immediately alerts a dog. And so, I decided, a coyote's howl may contain nuances so refined they cannot be distinguished by the human ear.

Then I thought: How farfetched you've become. Your mind has been infiltrated by demons of the dark. They are teasing you. With your reason they are making fun.

The deep dark of a silent night intrigues one with possibilities. It compounds the mystery, and a coyote's lonesome wail becomes a riddle.

Sound: so simple, yet so complex.

Each murmur is a clue to a deeper meaning. A breeze that sighs among green trembling leaves speaks to each of us in a different way. We hear in it the thing we want to hear.

To one it is pleasant and peaceful. To another it feels like rain is on the way. I may hear a whisper that sounds like a shout to you.

But some sounds I think we universally understand. They frighten or they soothe. They anger or they please. They sadden, too, and make us cry.

Sometimes we used to separate cows and calves overnight so we could tell in the morning when they were re-united which cow and calf belonged together.

All night long the cows would bawl, and their calves would answer back. They were scared and confused. They created a noisy symphony of despair that anyone could comprehend.

When the gate was finally opened the cows began sorting out their calves.

55

They talked to them in low, consoling voices. They soothed them with sounds I understood, even though I didn't understand a thing they said.

I could feel with them. Their relief was mine, and they expressed it in sounds that couldn't be mistaken -- even by someone who had never seen a cow.

Some sounds have that ability. They bridge the gap between us and other species. Mysteriously, we comprehend what we do not understand.

Anger is a dog's growl and pain is the way it yelps. Fear is a whine that grieves over the loss of comfort, and a bark that's filled with smiles is happy. And we know that.

And who could mistake the meaning of a feline's vicious hiss? Or confuse its gentle purr with anything but the complete contentment that it is.

The baby cries because it hurts, and the child squalls because it is mad. With soothing words mothers console as they wipe away the tears, and all is well again.

Each species responds with different sounds to those deep, deep feelings, and we seem to understand instinctively. Fear and anger, hurt and happiness are sounds we recognize.

There is an element, I think, that transcends sound itself. Perhaps it is an emotional VHF that operates on a band to which we were attuned long ago, in some misty past.

On a common denominator, it seems to me, we speak with the same voice. In common, we share some things with all life universally. In ways we refuse to recognize, we are one.

Flames Take Away
More Than A Home

A fire engine stood next to the curb while an angry cloud of smoke piled up against the sky. As lights flashed, traffic funneled into a single lane.

I expected to see firemen in a rush. I thought one or two would be climbing ladders so the blaze could be sprayed through holes they would chop into the roof.

But I thought wrong. After spraying a maple tree beside the burning house, they blasted the house next door with a jet of water to keep it cool.

People had gathered on the opposite side of the street to watch. They were sober. This was not a happy, roast-a-wienie kind of fire. There was something solemn about it, something sacrificial.

I, too, stopped to watch the firemen control the fire that had been set to burn the house. Of something it had become a victim: of progress, perhaps, or time.

Like a gaunt old animal it huddled there as the flames fed upon it. It reminded me of something stricken, something that hadn't been able to escape.

Across the front there was a porch. On either side of the door were two big holes that remained after the windows were removed. They reminded me of vacant-looking eyes, of sunken sockets filling with fire.

Then smoke started dribbling out of them, and around a column at the end of the porch it coiled dark ribbons as it left.

Feathery wisps of smoke began to curl upon the roof. Around a shingle withering in the heat, a lean red finger of fire reached out and it exploded in flame.

I had passed the house before, but I had never really seen it. Like we too often do, I didn't appreciate what it had been until it was being destroyed.

It had been a two-story house. Once it had been white, but the paint had blistered and broken. Steps that led up to the porch were gone, and half the railing around the edge had disappeared.

The yard sloped slightly down to meet the sidewalk. It was overgrown. In

57

the tangled grass were rusty cans and two beer bottles, the crop that flourishes when indifferences does the fertilizing.

Around the yard there was a picket fence that staggered off toward the corner where it had finally fallen. Once upon a time it had been painted white.

Hard times had come upon that old house and soon it would disappear. But what had it been? How many had lived there? How many nights had it waited for someone to come home? How many mornings had it watched them leave?

When houses are homes they become more than four walls, more than windows and doors. They become reflections of those who live there -- and those who had before.

Each one leaves a mark -- a hole in the wall where a picture was hung; a scar skidded across the floor by a runaway trike; a spot worn on the wall by a tipped-back chair.

Houses become museums where lives are displayed in fragments, in bits and pieces. Through the smoke I could see a patch of bright red wallpaper. And with it, I decided, someone had said: "There now, that looks better."

Houses live. They throb with life in glad times and sadden in times of grief. When things go right they sound with laughter, and console with quiet patience when they go wrong.

So what goes up in smoke when a house burns down? More, I think, than any book written can ever say.

The people who had clustered on the sidewalk across the street began to leave. I left, too. And as I walked away, I thought: Old houses show us more than we ever see.

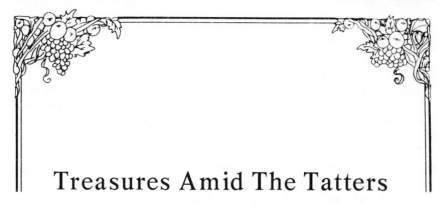

Treasures Amid The Tatters

Recently our daughter Leith, who will be a senior in high school this year, had some friends over one evening. They were in the living room, and I could hear them from the basement where I was fiddling around.

When I came up the stairs, I found a half a six-pack of pop sitting on the drainboard in the kitchen, a crumpled sack of potato chips and a jumbled array of candy and gum.

I stopped and looked at them. For a long time I looked at them because they seemed to symbolize something I couldn't put a finger on. They aroused a vague feeling like a memory that haunts because it only hints.

Finally, I went upstairs to bed. Before I went to sleep, I could hear Leith and her friends laughing and talking. Once in a while a blast of rock music hammered against the ceiling like demons on the loose.

The next morning the pop bottles were gone. A few tattered candy wrappers remained, and the crumpled potato chip sack was still there. It was empty. The party was over.

As I looked at them, I was suddenly reminded of another morning, an early September morning, 11 years before. Leith had just come down the stairs in her pajamas as she usually did because it scared her to be upstairs in the dark by herself.

Then she would lie down on the couch so she could see what was going on and I would get a blanket and cover her up. It was a ritual we went through.

As she curled up on the couch that morning, she said, "Daddy, make me a bed."

"But I can't," I said. "This morning you go to school -- for the first time."

Her eyes got wide as she looked up at me. She had forgotten.

But I hadn't. And as I stood there in the kitchen, I remembered the hollow way I felt as I watched her get up. As she went off to get dressed. I knew I had closed the book on a favorite chapter in my life.

Then I remembered Steve when he was probably a second-grader, and the

59

day he came home all enthused from school to tell us about a puppy some boy was going to give him.

"It's a mutt," he said. "That's what he called him, and that's the best kind, isn't it?"

"That's right," I told him. "Mutts are the best breed of dog there is."

When do you tell them? When do you decide that their blissful ignorance must come to an end? When do you introduce them to the realities you wish they could be spared forever?

And then there was Susan, and the time she had agreed to keep $3.00 for a friend. I don't remember why, but I remember that she lost the money. And I kidded her about the hazards of being a banker when she had to make it up.

I remembered as I stood there in the kitchen those other early mornings when Susan and Steve had come down the steps of the porch to crawl sleepily into the car for the ride to the bus that hauled them off to the strawberry fields.

As I watched, I hoped they would learn that happiness has to be enjoyed where it can be found -- that it has to be squeezed in, as it often is, among the hurts and the heartaches.

And that's what the crumpled potato chip sack and those tattered wrappers were symbols of. They were accessories that had gilded a moment of teenage happiness.

And so, on Father's Day, I believe that a man who hears the laughter of his children is truly blessed. It is a symphony that quickly ends, and he who hears it end on a happy note is indeed a lucky father.

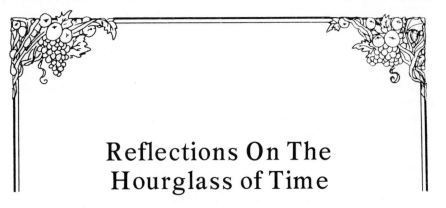

Reflections On The
Hourglass of Time

Why do I remember that little girl who ran around a barn late one windy afternoon with long blond hair splashing around her shoulders like water in the sun?

Why did the sight of her make me feel so hollow, so sad and lonely? What did I sense as she danced to a song that only she could hear?

Was it that? Was it knowing that I could never hear again the song she heard? Or see the sun so bright? Or feel the wind so fresh? Was it knowing that we never know how much we've lost until it's gone for good?

Why do I remember two boys who reached the crest of a hill just as the setting sun froze them for an instant in mid-stride: silhouettes standing at the edge of an unseen stage?

Were they the spirit of adventure personified? Were they youthful optimism going to see a play that had never been seen before? Were they curiosity, the wellspring of all wonder, seeking strange new sights?

Why do I remember the flowing, graceful cloud that resembled a grey jet plane against a dark red sky that a rising sun had set ablaze?

Was it because the cloud looked real enough to land at any airport, real enough to hear? Was it the latest, super-supersonic model?

I'm sure it was. And what a ride its passengers must have had. No film could have captured what they would have seen just before it dissolved in dawn's pale light to become a cloud again.

And the skunk I nearly hit the other night while it was shuffling across the road, a little explorer in black and white, why do I remember it? What could it share with me? Or me with it?

Did I want to go where it was going, to shuffle the way it shuffled? Did I want for an hour to be what a skunk will always be? Did I want to find out what headlights mean in the middle of a night that should be forever dark?

And the dog that was running down the highway, that crossed a bridge and turned left on the road I was taking -- why does he stick in my mind?

Where was he going at the early hour, running hard with a hot pink tongue lolling at the side of his mouth? Why did I slow down so I could follow, after he had pulled over to let me pass?

Why did he intrigue me so? Why had he become an enigma? Mesmerized, I watched.

He reminded me, I decided finally, of a rhythm, a flowing force that could not be stopped. Like rivers run over smooth, worn rocks he ran -- easily, without effort. He represented something I felt but did not comprehend.

Was it life in never-ending flow: life that begins in darkness and goes to a place we do not know? Was that the thought that kept me from passing when he pulled over?

And why had he crossed my path at that hour? Why had I crossed his? By being there he had become more than a dog returning from a night of wanderlust. He had become a mystery looking for an explanation as he galloped through my mind.

Was the old lady a mystery also, as she sat behind the window of a Greyhound bus that had wheezed up to the red light I was waiting on?

With a wizened, worn face, wrinkled as a paper sack that has been wadded up and thrown away, she looked down as I looked up. And when the bus began to pull away, I thought I saw her smile.

It was a wispy little smile, like a slow, indifferent ripple crossing a placid pond. But had she really smiled? Or had it just looked that way through a veil of diesel smoke?

She was swept along on a steely tide of traffic, and I will never know. And now I wonder: Will it make a difference after the dust of time has settled?

The album I look at is filled with snapshots I'll never understand.

Magic In Morning Silence

Late one afternoon as I rounded a corner not far from home, a wheel cover decided to go exploring on its own. It made a couple of long bounding leaps as it left the car, then shied off the road and spun into a ditch well padded with brush and berries.

It was getting to be a nuisance. That was the third time it had taken off in two days. Since it would soon be dark I decided to go back the next day and get it.

The next morning was Sunday and there wasn't much traffic, which made it convenient. The road where the wheel cover had taken off was narrow, and I had to walk quite a ways from an abandoned driveway where I parked the car.

It was a country road, one of those that doesn't get a whole lot of attention from maintenance crews because it isn't heavily traveled. It's kind of rough, with squinchy little shoulders and a faded white line that strays somewhat as it ambles down the center.

Nevertheless, it was a fine morning. A west wind blowing in from the ocean during the night had cleansed the air. But I didn't realize how clear it was until I looked up at the mountains that slumbered like big, dark humpbacked camels.

They looked like they had been cut out and pasted up against a milky white sky 'hat had been squeegeed clean of clouds and all other clutter. It was a scene that brought me to a stop. It looked like a time out of the past, before pollution had become a pestilence.

Then I noticed how still it was, how quiet, as though all movement had been arrested. I strained to hear and heard nothing. It seemed as though the very heartbeat of life had stopped to commemorate this special morning, so unruffled and serene.

My footsteps were the only sound. Then sheep I could not see began bleating softly, like gentle voices calling behind a fringe of trees growing

63

along the fences. It was the sound mankind had followed down through the centuries. It was a good sound.

In the field on the other side of the road, cattle were slowly getting to their feet. They were still drowsy and as they stretched, their shadows pulled away from them in the long slope of the rising sun like dark elastic bandages on the grass.

They watched me in curious contentment and I wondered what I was to them: a light disturbance rippling over the wrinkles in their brains, a strange blip on a screen of bovine bemusement?

I didn't arouse alarm, that was for sure. There was no place for it that morning -- no place for fear and anxiety. The world reserves some special moments for such serenity and that was such a moment. Time stopped then would be Paradise forever.

Then further back, higher up on another hill, I saw the coyote: a grey phantom drifting like a puff of smoke across the hillside. It stopped to investigate a hole, to explore it with a wary paw, then curved in slow trajectory toward the timber that had grown a dark line across the hill's high brow.

Slivers of sunlight were coming through the firs, and birds were beginning to chitter in the brush. But softly, respectfully, in tones deep silence is entitled to.

Then I slid down into the ditch, among vines with blackberries that autumn had dried into seedy little mummies, with thorns bared to protect them from the likes of me.

I finally spotted the wheel cover hunkering down among some vine maple where it hadn't expected to be seen, and I wished I hadn't. The search had been much more enjoyable than the find.

Living Under A Cloud Of Fear

Day after day we read about them in the newspapers: murders and muggings, robberies and rapes.

It creates a climate of fright, and after a while you wonder if it is safe to step outside your door -- in broad daylight. In some cities it isn't. Undeclared wars go on there 24 hours a day.

A sorry state of affairs, to be sure. It makes you wonder what the world is coming to. It makes you wonder if you're going to become another statistic in the latest crime report.

I was thinking about that the other day as I moseyed through the big fir trees that stand on a knoll at the back of our place. It came to mind as I watched a small wren bob nervously along the twisted limb of a small oak tree.

I don't know what it was looking for, but it never quit looking for a threat. Its head snapped from side to side as it sought to see everything at once. All the time it was teetering on the edge of flight.

Later that evening I was reminded of the same thing. I was working on a mowing machine beneath some oak trees when I heard a flock of crows migrating back to their nightly nesting grounds. I didn't move as they came swooping in for rest before they continued on their way.

The were caw-cawing back and forth, crow-talking the way they do when they feel secure. When I moved. all sound stopped except the breeze murmuring through the leaves.

Then a crow plummeted into flight from the top of a tree, and the others immediately followed. They had spotted the enemy, and they were gone. In an instant fear had overcome fatigue.

The sun was sinking into a pale pink flush on the horizon as I started for the house, and a robin went springing across the lawn. Birds have nothing to fear from me, and the robin had been around there long enough to know that. But it was ever alert to the danger that wild things continually anticipate.

If evolutionists are correct, I guess that's the way we once lived. I suppose we were afraid of our own shadows, which could instantly become an attacker in our minds. And the nights must have been fraught with fear, and all darkness, too.

As I thought about that wren, I tried to imagine what it would have been like to always feel unsafe. Could there have been contentment of any kind, I wondered, with unseen dangers constantly lurking at the edges of the mind?

Maybe birds and animals don't feel anything that corresponds to the fear we feel. Perhaps a perennial state of edginess is natural to them. It seems to be something most of them share, and for good reason.

Except for those so large and fierce nothing preys upon them, everything else becomes food for something stealthier, swifter, stronger. All that lives in the wild eventually becomes another's flesh. In an instant a bird's brash bounce becomes the cat's soft paw.

We, as human beings, have escaped that fate. We are no longer threatened by predators that will devour us on sight. We have risen above the law of fang and claw.

I'm not saying that it has been eliminated. Aggression, that deadly destructive behavior, is still with us. And today it appears to be breaking out of the legal stockade that once confined it.

For that reason doors we never used to worry about are locked when we go away. And in the night we awaken to strange sounds and lie in uneasy silence as we listen.

Nevertheless, despite locked doors and nighttime jitters, I feel lucky when I think of those crows, that robin and a tiny wren bobbing nervously on a small oak's twisted limb.

For them, unease is all the time.

A Family Of Trees

I know a place where four fir trees grew. They had been planted in a row beside the road. They were probably 2 feet in diameter.

I drove by them hundreds of times. I didn't realize how much of an impression they had made until each one assumed a personality of its own. At that moment, they became more than a row of Douglas firs standing on the other side of the ditch.

I'm not sure why we endow objects in nature with human characteristics. Maybe that's our way of trying to understand them. Perhaps we get lonely. Or do we subconsciously sense a kinship with them?

I don't know. But I do know that each of those trees became an individual in my imagination, and every time I passed that way, I got to know them better.

They were nearly the same size. They reminded me of quadruplets that had been nurtured by doting parents. But there the similarity ended.

One standing at the end of the row had long, sweeping limbs that reached out to everyone who went by. If a breeze was blowing, I could see it waving as I approached.

It was a happy tree. It never was downhearted, not even when it dripped with rain. I'm sure it was of the feminine gender. I considered it a sister of the others.

On hot days, she seemed to provide the most shade. I always supposed she was the coolest of the four, but I never stopped to find out. I wish I had.

Next to her stood a masculine fellow, with bark thicker and rougher than his sister's. He stood tall and straight. He looked as if he might have enjoyed a fight or a football game.

If his complexion hadn't been green, it would have been ruddy. He would have been a steelworker, or a logger. Pride flowed through his woody veins.

He didn't sway the way his sister did. He resisted the wind to demonstrate his strength. He was the macho type. When storms came, he liked to flex his muscles.

On the other side of him stood another sister -- at least she looked that way to me. Her branches seemed more fragile and lacy than did her sister's on the end. They reminded me of long and languid eyelashes.

She was the coy one. She was full of wiles. She flirted lightly with the breeze. She teased. Girls like her torment with averted eyes that suggest things they'll never say.

I always thought she would have been an ideal resting place for the serpent that tempted Eve. I have the feeling she would have done as Eve did if she'd had the chance.

Next to her stood the dour one. If they hadn't been the same size, I would have guessed that he was much older than the others.

I considered him the older brother. He had aged beyond his years as children often do who have been responsible for taking care of younger brothers and sisters.

He was phlegmatic, impassive. He didn't rock gracefully in the wind. His branches swung awkwardly, as though he were ill at ease. I don't think he had a sense of humor.

I never saw one there, but he would have made a good rest stop for buzzards. In his company they could have fueled up on the gloom that goes so well with their occupation.

And then one day they were gone: all four had been cut down. It came as a shock. It saddened me. I felt that I had lost four friends, friends who acted every day the way I knew they should.

The stumps are still there. But I don't see four stumps when I drive by; I see a cemetery.

Mountains Are Forever

Sometimes in the faint far off they look like illusions vaguely seen in a dream. Look away and they should be gone when you look back. But unlike things of dreams that shift soundlessly into something else, they remain there on the horizon, a sketch -- a jagged tracery left by an unseen hand.

They don't vanish like mirages growing misty in the mind. Like giant tapestries, like saw-toothed banners stretching across the sky, they remain. In the wily land of imagination they speak of mysteries, of secrets never told, of deep silence and a time no one knows. They speak of a past without a beginning and a future without an end.

Mountains are time arrested. They are time standing still. Or so it seems. But they are a paradox because they run wild with life.

They are a deer's quick-lifted head, and a bobcat's frozen glance. They are the slow flex of a sleepy cougar's paw, and a bright-eyed raccoon's slow swinging gait. They are a grouse exploding into flight at your approach, and the quick short run of quail for cover.

Mountains are never what they seem. They are as vibrant, as vital as a thrush's thrumming wing. But you may never know because they thrive with life that lasts longer when concealed.

Mountains are changeless change. With languid ease they switch their style. In green-leafed finery they dress for spring. Their meadows they spray with yellow and blue, those bloomy sockets that fill with nectar sought by bees that shoot like rifles through the busy buzzing air.

Then the steamy growth of summer, and the jointed reed-like reach of sprouts for length. And everywhere the swell of things erupting into life. The hurried rush, the headlong flurry of everything to become at once. And the mountains a haven, a home, where it can flourish.

Then brown comes to the meadows. And in a late day breeze the soft rustling rattle of life gone dry. For a moment, it seems, the days are tinged with autumn, and the haunting feeling that life is slipping silently away on those long melancholy afternoons.

Then one morning all is frosted white as angel food, and leaves begin to tinge with reds and rusts. The wind quickens, and the air turns chill. The clouds climb higher, and higher still, and with a sudden whooshing sweep of wind the first fresh snow flakes come riding in.

Like a hazy halo they whirl and swirl. Like tiny flighty creatures they settle lightly, tentatively, on this brown rock and that flat bare spot. Like powdered dust they lightly settle.

And accumulate like wide-flared skirts of white that wrap around each mountainous slope and make of every ridge and rise a pleat, and a ruffle of every canyon and each crevasse.

Upon those sloping shoulders it rests like a blouse of satiny white, with here and there a rock-ripped tear. But higher still, where vapors drift like steam on cloudless days, mountains rake the sky with great clawed peaks, and try with scissored edge to slice it wide.

All seasons touch the mountains with their special charm, but winter is the master decorator. With seamless white she clothes it all, and pulls it tight so it will fit. But tomorrow, if her mood should change, she will rearrange it with a windy whim.

With variety mountains inspire our awe and wonder. With each quick lift of face they tease us with illusion. But they are not a shadowy charade. They remain forever to enchant.

Season's Changes Part Of Natural Order

Who among us can accept the thought of his own demise? Even though we know the door will inevitably close, we struggle to keep it open.

Self-preservation, as we all know, is life's drive line. It propagates the species. It is the fang that slashes when it is threatened.

But shouldn't we be different, we, who watch each year's seasons pass? Shouldn't we be attuned to Nature's Cycle?

We've watched life that flourished in spring and summer dry up in autumn's chill before it died in winter's cold, cruel clutch. Don't we know that we too shall come and go? Aren't we aware that our passing is indelibly imprinted upon the Big Blueprint?

Of all the animals -- of all the living things -- only we know that's the way it is supposed to be. We know that seasons are a cycle that end but never do. And aren't we aware that infinity is their endlessness?

When summer ends we become more aware of time, it seems to me, and the way it is doled out to us in seasons. When autumn splashes yesterday's wilting green with rusty-red and gold, we stand for a moment in the silence and look for something we hope we cannot see.

And for a moment we know that what we've ignored we cannot escape. And before we turn away we see for one undeniable moment, the river where it ends.

Unlike the Indians of old who laid upon the ground so their aged, weakened bodies would be nearer their Mother Earth, we seek to immunize ourselves against time with pills and potions.

Unlike the Indians of old who drew close to the Earth as death approached, we deny the cycle that comes full circle. We close our eyes. Or look the other way.

We are distressed by life that ends in death, by seasons that come and go so soon. They destroy the sense of permanence that we seek. They arouse unease.

"It should mean more," we say, as leaves swirl like stricken sparrows through September's quiet afternoons.

"It's all so final," an old rancher said to me one afternoon as he sat on a bale of hay. "That's the reason I'm hoping for more than this."

As he turned them over he studied the palms of his hands. "Those calluses must mean something," he said. "They should be my ticket to the Promised Land."

He had earned them honestly. He had led an obedient life, and no one could accuse him of abusing his family, or neglecting a debt. He had worked hard. He had succeeded in doing what he wanted to do.

So why did he think he deserved more of a reward than a long fulfilling life? Wasn't that enough?

He massaged his chin with a finger and a thumb as he stared at a cow that was staring back at him. "I guess I'm tempted to want more," he said, "because of what I believe life could be."

"You don't think it can be found here?"

"I have no faith in people's ability to create a Paradise on Earth."

"But you believe there is one?"

"Winter is followed by spring, isn't it? And spring by summer?"

On the other side of every door that closes there is a new beginning, and that, I guess, is the lesson seasons tend to teach us.

The Meaning Of A Parade Hits Home

Late in the afternoon, as rain lightly sprinkled a crowd that had gathered along the sidewalks, the parade was forming at the edge of town.

It was supposed to start at 5 p.m., but the entries hadn't lined up on time, and it was already a half hour late.

But the delay didn't bother the people strung out along Main Street for the Fourth of July parade.

With foresight that others envied, some had brought umbrellas. A few had come with folding chairs that they sat up along the sidewalk.

As they settled back to wait, the older folks remembered other parades they had seen -- and times that looked better from a distance.

They talked about the Great Depression that had knocked the country's economy for a loop. And they remembered how it had been when it hadn't been very good at all.

But they had endured, and their belief in America had survived. And they had come on the Fourth of July to the main street of a little rural town to express their faith in a system they had supported through thick and thin.

As they patiently waited, the kids ran out into the street to see if the parade was coming. They were restless. They were nervous because young expectations want things to come on time.

With a shout, a wide-eyed boy of seven or eight announced that it was on its way, then scurried back to the curb and sat down. But he didn't stay there long because excitement is hard to sit upon.

The parade came slowly down the street. Veterans, dressed in uniforms that spend their time waiting in closets for the Fourth, were marching with the flag.

As the color guard approached it was appreciated with applause. As it passed, it was honored with a moment of silence that followed it like a ripple down the street.

Behind it came kids on bicycles masquerading as clowns and cowboys, monsters and mountain men. A few who didn't pretend to be anything at all joined the parade as it moved along because they wanted to be part of something.

Horses clopped down the street with riders sitting proudly in their saddles. Horses and history -- especially American history -- go together. Side by side they have gone down long, winding trails that crossed endless prairies and climbed steep mountain passes.

Some that seemed to possess a sense of history, expressed their pride with flashing eyes as they pranced and preened. Others that weren't so theatrically inclined plodded tiredly by. The world was not a stage on which they had come to perform.

Then came the marching band with drums and clashing cymbals. Twenty-two members, young and old, had combined to celebrate America's 200 years of independence. Voluntarily they had practiced so they could play on Independence Day.

They wore no uniforms. They were dressed in disarray. As it passed by, the band reminded me that freedom rests upon the shoulders of the people who support it voluntarily -- on the streets where they live, in the houses they call home.

Some Things
That Happened

Electricity Is A Shocking Experience

My brother introduced me to electricity when he talked me into touching the spark plug on an engine we were using to pump water. To use a tired old cliche in a literal sense, it was a shocking experience. I wondered then, and I wonder still, how anything as big as a basketball can run from the tips of your fingers to your shoulder and not tear your arm completely off.

By the time I decided it hadn't, Buggs had disappeared and I laid aside the pitchfork I was going to ventilate him with. I got even, though. The night the 12-gauge shotgun I was fooling with went off and blew a hole in the floor of the upstairs bedroom where he was sleeping shocked him into a state of upright, wide-eyed wakefulness.

"You might've hit me," he complained shakily as he came down the stairs. "If you'd aimed a little more to the right you would have."

I told him I would remember to do that next time. I never told him it was an accident. I don't want him to ever know.

That's not what I intended to talk about, but that's what electricity does. It confuses. It's a mystery and a riddle I'll never understand. How anything you cannot see can feel so much like something you should be able to is beyond my comprehension. It's sort of like eating a watermelon that doesn't exist so you can tell someone how good it really wasn't. I think there is a connection there, although a poor one, I'll admit.

Electricity doesn't affect everyone the same way. I knew a mechanic who tested the voltage of an engine by casually reaching in under the hood to grab a sparkplug wire. He would pulsate slightly every time it fired as though he were keeping time to a big bass drum. He didn't seem to suffer any lasting effects, but one time I heard him say that life was getting to be a drag.

"I can't get a charge out of anything anymore," he said, which led me to believe that he was losing his connection. I suppose it's like anything else: The more you get the more you need. If he isn't in a perpetual state of shock by now, I imagine he's looking for bigger and bigger charges.

I knew an electrician who was hooking up a transformer for a big electric motor. He was working outside in a slow gray drizzle when he crossed the wires. The jolt he took was something akin to the explosion of a hydrogen bomb, or a notice from IRS that your tax returns are going to be audited. That's the way he described it, anyway. And for a long time, he said, his mouth tasted copperish, like it was full of pennies.

When someone decided that that should have made him feel pretty rich, Red had shaken his head. On the contrary, it made him realize how really poor he was. If it had left a silvery taste in his mouth -- or a golden one -- he might have felt differently about it, he said with a grin about half as bright as an Abraham Lincoln one-cent piece.

Not long ago I was working on a hot water heater. I had disconnected the wire. To get it out of the way, I tossed it to one side. To get it out of the way some more, I tossed it to the other side. I kicked it around three or four days, until the water lines were hooked up. After the tank had been filled with water, I decided it was time to give it some juice. I picked up the wire and proceeded to cut the end off because it had been bent. There was a loud snapping noise, and a startling flash of fire. When I could see again, I checked the wire pliers I had been using. They looked sort of funny with their jaws burnt out.

What gets me is this: I knew I had shut off the electricity to that line. With 220 volts I don't care to take chances. But it wasn't off, that was for sure. It didn't shock me because the pliers had shorted the current into the ground wire. However, just thinking about the jolt I could have gotten gave me quite a thrill. For once I was happy to settle for less than the real thing. I'm not wired for 220, of that I'm sure.

A Lie That Wasn't Worth Living

When I was a kid I had a .22 rifle, I shot it until the barrel leaded up and wouldn't shoot anymore. After I had pestered Grandad for a month or more, he agreed to let me use his .410 shotgun once in a while.

It wasn't much of a jump from a .22 rifle to a .410, so I had no qualms about shooting Granddad's gun. But I was leery of 12-gauge shotguns. I knew how hard they kicked.

I had seen how black and blue my dad's shoulder turned after he had been out hunting with his long-barreled 12-gauge. But what really made me leery was the single barrelled 12-gauge owned by my brother Buggs, who was four years older than I was.

It was so light it shot as hard backward as it did forward. He failed to hold it tight one time and when he pulled the trigger the stock reared up and slapped him in the mouth. It bled, and for two days his lip was swollen.

The next time he fired it, he hung on as though his life depended on it. To keep from seeing the disaster that might result, I think he closed his eyes. That may have been the reason he so often hit what he was aiming at.

I didn't want to shoot a 12-gauge gun. I was scared. I'll admit it now, but I wouldn't have then. When I was asked if I wanted to, I could usually come up with an arm too sore to chance it at the moment.

With excuses galore I tried to maintain an illusion of bravery without revealing the cowardly truth. Buggs knew what I was doing and he wouldn't let me forget it. But he didn't tell because I knew some things about him that he didn't want broadcast. Sometimes it takes an uneasy balance to maintain the status quo.

But the day was coming. Sooner or later I would be forced to pull the trigger on one of those blunderbusses, and I was dreading it. I wondered how bad a broken shoulder hurt. And how long it would be, I wondered, before I could eat with a broken jaw.

I'm not sure why, but one day I went to the neighbors. I suppose I was on

77

some sort of errand. If I had known what was going to happen, I would have stayed at home.

When I got there, Ralph was out in the yard. He was 15 or 16 -- five or six years older than I was. Slanting up against a chopping block next to the wood pile was his 12-gauge shotgun.

When I saw it, my heartbeat quickened. I had a feeling that something was going to happen. I had a premonition, as they say.

Ralph told me he was going hunting, and as he picked up his gun I complimented him on it. He nodded as his hand slid lovingly down the barrel. He liked it better than he did Buggs', he said, because it was heavier and didn't kick as hard. I told him I knew exactly what he meant.

"Have you shot his?" he asked.

"A few times," I said.

"Then you've got to try mine to see how much difference there is."

I had trapped myself and pride wouldn't let me back out. My hands trembled as I reached for the gun. I didn't shoot at anything -- I just swung up and blazed away with my eyes closed.

The stock bucked against my shoulder, but nothing broke. I didn't even hurt. Slowly I opened my eyes. I was dumbfounded.

There was an amused glimmer in Ralph's eyes when I handed him his gun. He knew then I had never fired a 12-gauge before.

"Now you better go home and try your brother's so you can see how much difference there really is," he said. He grinned as he shouldered his gun and walked away.

Isn't it strange, the lengths we'll go to live a lie?

Out From Behind Closed Doors

I was a fan of country and western music back when it was a stigma, a taint upon your reputation; upon your ancestry, and your place of birth. You tried to conceal it the way you would an extra finger, or a tattoo that flaunted a name that wasn't your wife's.

If you played country-western on your car radio you did so on the sly -- with the volume turned way down and a sophisticated citified look on your face so no one would surmise. But there were ways to tell.

If you saw a car creeping along a crowded street on a hot summery day with the windows rolled up and sweat running off the driver's face, you could almost be sure you'd spotted a CW junkie. Chances are the "Great Speckled Bird" had just been freed and he was listening as it soared in the torrid tomb his car had become. A closet fan of country-western didn't have an easy time.

One night in a small gathering where I didn't belong, music was mentioned. The people there weren't country-western types. They were cultured people, whose conversations were sprinkled with Bachs and Beethovens and Chopin in the Fifth. When I heard someone say "counterpoint," I cringed. When I heard something that sounded like "contrapuntal," I began slinking off.

Before I got away someone said, "Hee Haw," and a great wave of hee haws rippled around the room. I slunk to the door, and cursed myself for not telling those people how country-western music touches something deep down and elemental in the soul that cannot be expressed, that all their slanderous remarks could not destroy. I wanted to tell them that it spoke of verities: of love and death and suffering and sadness...

But I gritted my teeth in silence until I was driving home. Then I let them have it. I told those snobs all the things I had been thinking. Buck and Roy would have been proud of me. I wish someone had been there to listen.

I've heard it said that country music is sad. I won't deny that. I won't even try. Some country-western songs have reason to be. They have suffered immeasurably. They have been knocked out of tune by more off-key, guitar-picking singers than Carter has pills. I've heard some of the better ones. I had a friend who was one of the best. That I should still like country music is a miracle, considering the hours I've listened to its agonized wail of anguish.

Sammie had what it took to be a success: good looks, good personality, poise and confidence, plus a hint of arrogance. He lacked but two things: talent and the humility to realize that it wasn't there. He knew that if he endured long enough -- and persisted hard enough -- he was going to make it all the way to the mecca of country music: the Grand Ole Opry in Nashville.

I can tell you for sure that he persisted. His trusty guitar was ever at the ready. You didn't have to waste time persuading him to play. You couldn't have stopped him with a pair of machine guns. Sometimes a song he had composed himself would be included in his repertoire. Such blessings were almost more than one could stand.

I could take those. But when he took off on some of the classics, it really hurt. I tried not to listen. Something deep down and elemental in my soul pleaded for relief.

The Wabash Cannon Ball was one of Sammy's frequent victims. He could de-rail that fine old flyer before it had cleared the station. When he sounded the whistle, it sounded like a plea for mercy. If he hadn't been a friend I would have laced his fingers together with strings snatched from his own guitar.

Failure repeated often enough punctures the most persistent ego, and Sammie's finally deflated. It's too bad. He would have made it big if he had hung on. Discord finally came into its own. For the last few years it has been riding high on the charts.

I felt sorry for him, but I was relieved when he laid his guitar away. If he had made it to Nashville, fans of country music might still be listening behind closed doors.

Just Stringing Along

While walking across a small hayfield I saw what I thought was a string lying on top of the grass. It was 200 feet away from the highway that runs by our place, and I assumed the wind had blown it there after it had been thrown from a passing car.

But I soon changed my mind. Even though I don't know how long strings are supposed to be, I knew it was longer -- lots longer -- than most strings are. I yanked on it a couple of times but it wouldn't come free. It was fast on both ends.

From the center of our field it ran toward our neighbor's pasture and crossed the fence that separates our places. From there I could see it swooping like a tiny green wire up into a fir tree 100 feet farther on. When I pulled I could see branches jerking in the top of the tree. It finally broke free, but it was tough stuff. It took a real pull before it parted.

I began rolling it up as I walked back toward our barn. It didn't seem to have an end. It crossed the fence next to the barn, and threaded its way across a lot before it rose gracefully into an oak tree near the house. There it had become tangled. When I tried to pull it free it broke.

At first I thought it was the string from a kite some kid had lost. But there was no sign of a kite in the oak tree. And there was none in the fir trees across the fence in our neighbor's pasture because I went back to see.

As I tramped across the field it occurred to me that I had undoubtedly discovered the beginning of a space age spider's giant web.

I assumed it had evolved in one of NASA's think tanks. And I decided the one whose web I'd found had been a rudimentary model on a test run that had been aborted for some secret reason.

It is just the beginning, I thought. As future generations were genetically engineered, I figured NASA would be able to create spiders big enough to spin webs as large as hawsers on a ship.

It was really an exciting breakthrough. There would no longer be any doubt about our supremacy in space. The Russians had better take note, I thought. With webs such as those it would be a simple matter to net their satellites the way most people net butterflies.

But that wouldn't be their only practical use. They could also be used as giant seines to fish the oceans clean. And just think what one sweep across the Pacific from San Francisco to Hawaii might yield. There would be fish, millions of them probably, of who knows how many varieties. And seals and whales, a sun-tanned surfer or two, a Soviet fishing fleet taken off the Oregon coast, 1,500 feet of trans-oceanic telephone line and Lord knows how many interrupted long distance calls. It didn't look like Ma Bell was going to be too happy.

It would be quite a haul, no doubt. And when all those fish had been deposited on the outskirts of town, Honolulu would enjoy the distinction of being the last place anyone would want to live.

But one of the world's greatest worries would be eliminated. By depleting the sea of all its life in one fell swoop, we wouldn't have to agonize about doing it over a longer period the way we're doing now.

But the real treasures would be taken during a sweep of the South Pacific. Off the bottom would come battleships, great carriers, destroyers and cruisers, airplanes and subs. There would be enough to convert Australia into one great museum -- a memorial -- to Ares, the mythological god of war, at whose alter mankind worships with such destructive insanity.

When I told my wife, Jeannie, about the string, it didn't take her long to unravel my theory. It was a fishing line, she said, that had dropped off some fisherman's boat. Since it is spring, she explained, a bird picked up one end of the line to build a nest with. And it was so light, the bird had not rouble stringing it across the field and two fences before it got tangled up in the trees. Undoubtedly, Jeannie is right. She always is.

But I'll bet that fisherman was surprised when he found his line missing. I bet he would be even more surprised if he knew what a monstrous breed of spiders he almost created.

Cause And Effect

I learned about cause and effect when Granddad decided to pull out a gnarled stump with a team of horses. He thought it would be a snap. It had stood so long at the edge of the pasture he figured its roots had rotted off.

But they hadn't, and the chain he was going to yank it out with broke when the horses tightened up on it. "By dogs," he said, "it's stouter'n it looks."

I was just a kid, and he sent me to the barn for another chain. With one end over my shoulder, I drug it back to him. It was so heavy, I didn't figure it would break. Granddad was of the same opinion.

"By dogs, if that'un breaks," he said, "I reckon we'll have to blast." After we had hooked it up, he picked up the reins and spoke to the horses.

As they leaned into their collars, the stump slowly began to tip. Then the doubletree snapped, and the horses went to their knees from pulling so hard.

Granddad frowned. He seasoned the air with tobacco juice and looked the situation over. "I reckon we could get a stouter doubletree," he said, "but if we did, the harness'ud most likely pull apart, 'n if we got a heavier harness, the horses'd probably bust a gut."

After he had talked it all out logically, he decided it would be best to give rot a little more time to weaken the roots. "Nother two or three years," he said, "'n it'll likely fall over."

I gathered up the chain, and he unhitched all but one of the tugs so the horses could drag the broken doubletree back to the barn.

"Funny," he said, as we trudged along behind them, "how one damn thing follows another, and each one of 'em is worse than the one before that.

He was sure enough right. Every cause has an effect. One young carpenter I know will attest to that. He was literally showered with effects.

While remodeling a commercial building, he had to tear out some sheetrock in a ceiling so he could put in headers to support a heavy light fixture.

83

Things weren't going as smoothly as he wanted them to, and he started swinging a little wildly with the crowbar he was using. With one exuberant swing he decapitated an overhead sprinkler that was supposed to go off when a fire started.

Immediately it doused him -- and the hallway in which he was working, and a room or two on either side of it. By the time he found a way to shut it off, a lively little stream was gurgling happily around his feet.

The contractor he worked for wasn't too happy because the mess had to be cleaned up at his expense. If I remember correctly, some carpeting had to be replaced, and some walls had to be repainted.

When the young craftsman finally got back to doing what he was supposed to have already done, he gave the sprinkler a wide berth. He ignored it. He didn't want anything more to do with it.

It was a cold morning, and he took a heater to work with him. It was one of those kerosene-burning, rocket-shaped jobs that sound like a 747 taking off when they are going full blast.

Since he was working on the ceiling, he had to stand on a small ladder. To keep warm, he propped the front of the heater up so it would blow heat in his direction.

He was getting along fine, and then it happened -- again. The blast from the heater set the sprinkler off and once more he took a shower, as did the hallway and the walls.

I'm sure he would have agreed with Granddad when he said: "Funny how one damn thing follows another" ... with one exception. He may have had a little trouble with the part about it being funny.

An Angry Recoil

They are supposed to be lifeless, inanimate objects without vestige of pulse or protoplasm. But don't believe it. That's propaganda desseminated to deceive the unwary.

When plastic garden hose gets cold it lives; I'll guarantee it. I found out not long ago when I decided to coil up one I had used last fall to wash the car.

I was motivated by a desire to procrastinate no longer. Had I known how things were going to turn out, I wouldn't have taken myself so seriously.

It was a brisk, chilly morning and everything was furry with frost. In the early morning sun the lawn sparkled like a swatch of green velvet sprinkled with a million jewels.

I remembered dragging the hose up next to the fence when I was through so it wouldn't be in the way. I finally found it stretched out in the grass that had just about obscured it.

It began resisting immediately. When I tried to pull it out on the driveway it wrapped itself around a fence post. I gave it a yank, and it hooked the fence with a brass fitting on one end. It wouldn't let go until it had been twisted loose.

I should have given up then. I should have dragged it back along the fence and let the grass have it. By now it would be out of sight and out of mind. Alas, I did not. I had paid for it, and it was going to obey.

Not willingly however, it flexed like a long green plastic snake when I started bending it into a coil. The tighter I coiled, the more contorted it became. While I was winding up three circles about two feet in diameter, it writhed around my legs like a 50-foot boa constrictor.

I hadn't realized it was so cold and I hadn't worn gloves. My hands were beginning to get numb and I was in too much of a hurry when...

SPLATT!

I thought I had been smacked with an old soupbone when the end of the hose slipped out of my hand and slapped me in the face.

My grip slipped when it hit me and the coils I was holding in my hands

85

took off like hula hoops. When they finally came to rest, they formed two angry circles around my feet.

I kicked at them as I went to get some gloves, and they snapped back as I walked off. It wasn't lifeless, as you can see. A Walt Disney cartoon couldn't have been more animated.

Before I started in again, I went to the barn and got some twine I had cut off a bale of hay. This time it wasn't going to get away. I would hog tie the hose as I went along.

As soon as I had rounded up the first coil, I tied it in place. I didn't use any fancy nautical knots, either. No rolling bowlines for it. I secured it with good old hard-to-untie granny knots, reefed up snug and tight.

Each coil I tied. And each one I tied with the same old granny knot. If a surgical incision had been tied the way I tied that hose, the stitches would have lasted longer than the patient.

The hose is hanging in the shed now, and round and round it goes. I don't think I'll ever untie it. I'll use it the way it is. After going through all those circles the water should come out round enough to roll wherever I want it to go.

Auto Lemons Should Be Hauled Into Court

"Yamhill County vs. one 1978 Chrysler LeBaron and others."

When I read that in the court records of the Statesmen-Journal the other day, I thought: "What a fine idea."

I still think it is. There's nothing I would like better than a chance to sue a couple of cars I've owned. I'd charge them with everything but the battery.

One was a first-class lemon. It wasn't supposed to be. When I bought it, I was told that it had been driven by a kindly old lady who rode a bicycle wherever she went.

Low mileage it had. It also had a bad disposition. As spoiled as it was, I suppose I should have anticipated that. But I don't like to anticipate a bad deal any better than the next guy.

When I went back and complained to the salesman, he said: "You've got to give it time to adjust. It's a one-owner car. It's been discriminating, if you know what I mean."

I never had much luck going back on the previous owner when I got stung in a car deal. Even when I got their heartfelt sympathy it didn't go far. You couldn't buy a sparkplug with a barrel of it.

That's the reason I was happy to see that lawsuit filed against that LeBaron. I'm not sure what it was charged with, but if it acted like that car I had, it was guilty. A day in court was the best thing that could happen to it.

Providing it gets to court. The dockets are so full it may become a classic before it ever comes to trial. If what you sue is a hunk of junk that becomes a classic during a long delay, you'll probably come out on the short end of things.

I wish time didn't play such a big part in legal matters. It grieves me to think that the statute of limitations has run out and I'll never be able to sue that ornery auto I owned.

I didn't expect to feel that way when I bought it. It looked like a gem: all freshly painted in battleship grey with bright red wheels and small, shiny

87

bright-eyed hubcaps. It looked like a happy little thing that wanted nothing more than a good time.

Never was anything so deceptive. Under that shiny exterior a bitter little hellion skulked. It never wanted to go where I wanted to. And it never, never wanted to go when I did.

As soon as I stepped on the starter it would begin to whine. And it would whine until it had just about exhausted its tired old battery. Then it would start.

But for one reason only: to let me know how badly it felt. I have never heard such coughing and wheezing and long drawn-out strangling sounds as it emitted. Its lungs must have been in awful shape.

It would shudder and shake and its tailpipe would vibrate alarmingly. It went through such awful contortions I often thought that it should have been in an intensive care unit.

Even if I sued, I don't think I would have won. If it had performed for the judge the way it performed for me very morning, I would have been out of luck. He would have charged me with auto abuse in the first degree.

That's what I don't like about pampered automobiles. They get the idea that they deserve more than a good kick in the tires occasionally.

Miracle Potions Still Needed

I thought medical science was progressing, but I'm about to change my mind. A paper that was published in Shaniko, Oregon, which was once the wool capital of the world, has aroused my doubts.

On Thursday, August 28, 1902, the Shaniko Leader included this article among news items appearing on Page 1:

" 'Last March I had as a patient a young lady of 16 years of age, who had a very bad attack of dysentery. Everything I prescribed for her proved ineffectual, and she was growing worse every hour.

" 'Her parents were sure she would die. She had become so weak she could not turn over in bed.' "

Then, wrote the good doctor, he thought of "Chamberlain's Colic, Cholera and Diarrhea Remedy," and as a last resort, prescribed it.

" 'The most wonderful result was effected,' he added. 'Within eight hours she was feeling much better; inside of three days she was upon her feet, and at the end of the week she was entirely well.' "

That remarkable potion was "For Sale at Dr. S.L. Perkins' Drugstore," right in the heart of downtown Shaniko.

What has happened to that potent elixir? Why isn't around still, effecting those most wonderful results?

Was it too great a threat? Did the medical profession fear that it would be replaced by such magic potions?

If so, this, which also appeared on the Leader's front page, did nothing to allay those fears:

"All Sadieville, Ky., was curious to learn the cause of the vast improvement in the health of Mrs. S.P. Whitaker, who had for a long time endured untold suffering from chronic bronchial trouble.

" 'It's all due to Dr. King's New Discovery,' writes her husband. 'It completely cured her and also cured our little granddaughter of whooping cough.'

" 'It positively cures coughs, colds, LaGripe, bronchitis, all throat and lung troubles. Guaranteed bottles 50 cents and $1.00. Trial bottles free at Dr. S.L. Perkins' drug store.' "

In 1902, there wasn't an ailment known to man that couldn't be cured quickly, painlessly and permanently. And "Kodol," which was advertised in bold black letters on the Leader's back page, possessed great curative powers.

It was a "Dyspepsia Cure," and this is the way it was described:

"Digest what you eat. This preparation contains all of the digestants and digests all kinds of food. It gives instant relief and never fails to cure. It allows you to eat all the food you want.

"The more sensitive stomachs can take it. By its use many thousands of dyspeptics have been cured after everything else failed. Is unequalled for stomach. Children with weak stomachs thrive on it. First dose relieves. Diet unnecessary."

And the $1.00 bottle contained 2½ times more than the 50-cent size.

"The Home Gold Cure" was advertised in the same issue of the Leader. It was described as "an ingenious treatment by which drunkards are being cured daily in spite of themselves."

"No noxious doses," said the ad. "No weakening of the nerves. A pleasant and positive cure of the liquor habit."

And where, I want to know, can anything be found today that will "work wonders on sores, bruises, skin eruptions, cuts, burns, scalds and piles?"

"Bucklen's Arnica Salve" would. It only costs 25 cents, said the Leader, and it was "guaranteed to cure."

Just think what a giant step forward the medical profession could take -- once it catches up with its miraculous past.

Stepping Out With A Cure

Simplicity is best, I sincerely believe that. There's no need to complicate things with a plethora of grandiloquent theories and hypothetical prognostications. That's especially true where the human anatomy is concerned.

I didn't realize how simple it was until I saw a pair of human feet illustrated in an advertisement the other day. I didn't know until then that our feet are directly connected to the vital organs of our bodies. But I guess they are.

By the illustrator's reckoning, the four smaller toes on each foot are hooked to the sinuses. Just behind them are areas responsive to the ears, eyes and neck. The solar plexus, the heart, the stomach and pancreas, gall bladder and spleen -- all are connected to specific spots on the soles of our feet.

That's simplicity at its best. No $1,000 examinations are required to pinpoint our aches and pains. No needling with needles, no tests to undergo. One little caress and the spleen becomes less splenetic. One quick massage and relief is on the way.

A thing I hadn't understood came clear after seeing that. I've always wondered why a person's head hurt after standing all night at a bar drinking double shots. Now I think I know.

I've been told that drinkers tend to tip forward in direct proportion to the amount they've drunk. Undoubtedly, that inclined posture puts undue pressure on the tips of their big toes, which are wired directly to their brains.

So it's no wonder their heads hammer and throb the next morning. In reality, they've been standing on them with their own two feet. And that, as any hungover drinker will tell you, feels like it must have been quite a feat.

As you can see, diagnosis becomes a simple matter once you get used to it. Treatment of normal aches and pains used to be just as simple. When poultices were in vogue, strains and sprains presented no problem at all.

The kind of poultices I became acquainted with as a kid were made of cloth

91

on which something was applied that would relieve swelling and inflammation when wrapped tightly around an offending limb.

Bread and milk were a favorite. The ingredients were usually handy, and they were easy to prepare. They were soft and soothing -- and sort of squishy.

When they were fresh, every strange dog in the country would line up behind you with saliva drooling off his tongue. But your popularity diminished in short order when the milk began to sour. Nothing will curdle a friendship quicker.

Poultices could be made of most anything. All sorts of concoctions were brewed up from goose grease, duck down, and I don't remember what all. Cow manure was not to be sneezed at when it came to strains and sprains too severe for bread and milk to handle.

In fact, it was difficult to sneeze at all while holding your nose, but that rich aroma promoted rapid recovery. When your only thought was of that breath of fresh air hovering like an elusive halo just beyond the range of your quivering proboscis, getting well seemed to be the only logical alternative.

However, not all effective remedies originated in our sorefooted past. A friend of mine recently came up with a novel cure for the common cold. He swears by it.

He heard somewhere that cold germs can't survive temperatures lower than 40 degrees Fahrenheit. I don't know where he got his information but he's invested his faith in it.

When he gets the sniffles, he sticks his head in the freezing compartment of his refrigerator and the chilled air he breathes kills the germs. He's convinced of that. "And in no time at all," he says, "I'm cured."

And that, as far as I'm concerned, reveals how truly simple things can be.

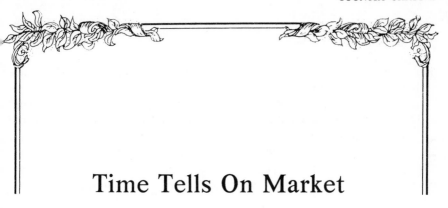

Time Tells On Market

Johnny Cash was there on a dusty record album lying upon a cluttered table top. This wasn't the Johnny Cash we see today. He was young when that picture was taken, slim and trim. He was putting in an appearance from the past.

So was the record. Songs that had been played and played 25 years ago drifted slowly back in memory time. "Ring of Fire" floated by like a whiff of smoke.

Next to the record album stood a stack of books. "Skinny ones, 25 cents," said the sign. "Fat ones 50 cents." If Jack Spratt could read no fat, and his wife could read no lean, they would have been in luck where literature sold by size -- and cheap enough for all to enjoy.

But there was no line of eager buyers. Literature, it appeared, had come upon hard times. A bankrupt Shakespeare would have mourned his loss of popularity as he aged upon the shelf.

Across the aisle stood an old volume in faded red. The author was Irvin S. Cobb. He was a Kentuckian, a humorist, who wove a tapestry of laughter around his characters.

In that faded volume he had created a fictitious judge so humor could prove itself in a court of law where readers served as jurors. It was published in 1916. Price: $3.00.

"Apple Blossom Time" was all dressed up in a cover of bright sheet music just around the corner. "Sweet Adeline" was there, too. But what are notes that are never played? A stingy silence refused to answer.

If it could have talked, an old flatiron abandoned in a corner would have told some tales. It had seen some hot times. In its day it had probably been a scorcher.

But it would see no more ironing boards. It had reached trail's end. Not even a price remained. Where it had been there was a smudge. The market for old irons had gone flat.

An ancient kerosene lamp cast a shadow on a table top. It had no wick. It

93

would light the way no more. In darkness it would spend the nights it once had brightened.

Under a jumble of knicknacks a manual for a 1951 Ford was buried. It was illustrated with engines large and small. Gears and gauges, crankshaft and carburetor were well defined. "Sale price $1."

In a wooden case a small Royal typewriter waited for a buyer. It was priced at $29.95. On paper rolled around the platen someone had typed: "This is a good buy." But not good enough for the writer of that line.

He may have missed a golden opportunity. It looked to be in top condition. The great American novel may have been lying dormant inside its glossy case. A fat one may have been there, too, and who knows how many skinny ones.

A sewing machine stood on a nearby table with all of its attachments exposed. It tried hard to look as sleek and streamlined as the models that had replaced it, but it couldn't conceal its obsolescence. Out-of-style is hard to hide.

On a hanger dangling from a wire a Navy uniform hung listlessly. The sleeves were loose and limp. It looked like it was waiting for a war that hadn't happened. Or had fought in one that hadn't been. Whatever the reason, it had missed the ship and all the glory.

Over there was a set of ancient wrenches, shaped like rusty S's. And what was that: that short cylinder to which four pins were welded? Where was Paul Harvey with "The Rest of the Story?"

Flea markets surround us with a thousand yesterdays. They are rear-view mirrors that reflect upon that mysterious thing called time, which slowly gilds the new with age and consigns it to antiquity.

The Things People Do

Taking The Easy Way Out

My arrival was announced by three big, loud-mouthed dogs, and a couple that weren't quite as loud because they weren't quite as big. They whipped like shaggy whirlwinds among the kids that seemed to come from everywhere to watch with solemn shyness as I got out of the pickup.

There was a bunch of them. They were all sizes. They were all blonde and blue-eyed and ranged in hue from tattle-tale gray to darker shades of dinginess. It didn't look like they had seen a bar of soap for a long time. Mr. Lifebuoy would have chortled with glee at the sight of them.

I thought maybe they had run out of water, but they hadn't. The tank the cattle drank from was full. There was even a mudhole beside it where water had overflowed. As I glanced at the kids, I wondered why it hadn't been put to better use.

Their dad was a long, lean slow-talking fellow, who wore an old straw hat. When he heard the dogs barking he sauntered out of the chicken house behind the barn.

He was a pleasant sort of fellow, and the kids seemed to love him. When he came to a stop they crowded around his legs, pulled at his hands and swung on the rear pockets of the bib overalls he wore.

When he found out I was there to look at some cattle he wanted to sell, he pulled out a sack of tobacco and rolled a cigarette.

"Yeah," he said, as he puffed up a thoughtful cloud of smoke, "I got a few old rinds I been thinking about selling. I'll send the kids up to run 'em down."

With the dogs yapping as they started up the hill, they reminded me of ragged little rabbits running in the sun. As they disappeared among the oaks growing higher up the hill, I thought about pictures of natives I had seen in National Geographic magazine.

"Like some lemonade?" he asked, as he glanced over his shoulder at the house, where his wife was watching from the porch.

I shook my head. I'm not squeamish, but what I could see of the kitchen through the open door behind her quenched my thirst, even though it was a hot day.

In a little while the cattle came lumbering down off the hill, with their tails snapping angrily at the flies hovering over them. We moved over to the corral, and he closed it with a loose, limp gate of rusted barbed wire as soon as the kids and the cattle were inside.

The dogs flopped in the shade of the barn with their tongues lolling out, and the kids watched as their dad moseyed through the cattle and showed me the ones he wanted to sell.

But they soon tired of that, and as they raced across the corral in search of something more exciting, one of the bigger ones shoved one of the smaller boys into the mudhole next to the water tank. As he went down, he let out a squall.

His dad walked over and helped him to his feet. After he had looked him over, he led him up to the tank. With water he dipped out with his hand, he tried to wash the mud off the squirming little guy, but he wasn't having much luck.

"It's might near as easy to make a new one as it is to clean up one of the old ones," he said with a rueful grin.

I didn't say so, but it looked to me like he had been taking the easy way out long enough.

Inheritances Bring Out The Worst

It occurred to me the other day that a relationship exists between inheritances and reincarnation. At least, it seems that way and I offer this as evidence.

A man who had a daughter as his only heir owned a large and prosperous ranch. When he died he willed it to her. It would remain hers, his will stipulated, as long as she remained single. If she married, it passed to a distant relative.

She never married, which may have been one of the smartest things she ever did, considering the fate of most marriages today, and the ranch remained hers. But her father had deprived her by denying her the right of choice.

No, that's not right. He didn't deny her a choice, he just made choosing more difficult. And I'm inclined to believe she made the right one. I would rather have a good ranch than a husband any day. But I'll admit that I may be prejudiced: I like ranches.

Anyway, that's what she did, and I've tried to see things from her father's viewpoint. I've tried to live in his head -- look through his eyes -- but for the life of me I can't see the things he saw.

I can only believe that he believed in reincarnation. And his mind must have been buzzing with the thought that as long as the ranch belonged to his daughter he had a pretty good chance of sweet talking her out of it when he was recycled.

But his plans went astray, if that's what he had in mind. The years rolled by and his daughter grew old. Then she died, and he still hadn't put in an appearance.

I'm not sure what happened to the ranch, but it definitely passed beyond his control. If there is any justice in this world, it only seems right that he should have been reincarnated as the pesky mosquito his daughter slapped out of existence one warm summer evening as she sat alone on the porch.

Inheritances create problems, that's for sure. If there is any logic in life, it seems to disappear when the time comes to divide an estate. When palms begin to itch with greed, reason runs for cover.

Even if they weren't created to keep greed from dying out, inheritances have done a fine job of it. Families squabbling over who gets what when a relative dies have feathered more than one lawyer's nest.

What one has accumulated, others can't wait to divvy up -- as long as they get a big slice of the pie. And they're frequently prepared to slice up anyone who gets in their way.

Inheritances have produced more chicanery than the U.N. General Assembly, which is no slouch. And the real infighting begins before the will has even been read.

A dish, a piece of crystal, an old clock, a bent spoon -- even a lock of Suzy's hair -- will sometimes produce enough fuel to send flames of greed flaring high into the sky. And someone usually gets singed before they die down.

Lying, cheating and stealing are considered justifiable means to the end, which is simply plundering when stripped of: "But Momma said I was to get it," which is vehemently denied by: "I never heard her say no such a thing," which opens the door for this blast: "You're always trying to get something for nothing, aren't you?"

It's amazing the different things heirs are told -- to hear them tell it. I heard three members of the same family declare with all the sincerity that greed can muster that they had each been promised the same thing an untold number of times by their dear, departed mother.

It's too bad she couldn't have risen from the grave and snatched it away. If we are reincarnated, I don't imagine she'll elect to return as a human being after witnessing that. She might be smart if she didn't elect to return at all.

If we could just take it all with us when we go, we could solve a lot of problems. Who do you suppose I should talk to about that?

Beware Of The Love Bug

This is a tale about love. It must have been. Nothing makes people act the way love does.

It began when a friend of mine met Mary. Something flashed between them the first time they met, and the sparks continued to fly for a long time afterward.

Mary didn't like me. She didn't want Tim to have any close friends. If she was going to be his, she wanted him to be hers. Naturally, my feelings toward Mary weren't of the tenderest sort.

They got married, but they didn't waste much time on trust and devotion. They got right down to making life miserable for each other. And a marriage fertilized with distrust, suspicion and jealousy will produce a fine crop of misery.

Some of their domestic wars were real rip snorters. Then they split up, and went back together again. Then they broke up again, reconciled, and gave it another go. When another war broke out, they called it quits.

For good, said Tim. No more. He was through. He was all done with her. Since neither of us had any money to speak of, we decided to share an apartment. We found one, a cheap little place, in a rundown section of town.

It was owned by an old couple, who had remodeled their home to create an apartment for additional income. It was small, but it was spic and span. And they were fine folks. What we didn't have in the way of pots and pans they loaned us.

By sharing expenses, the cost of living wasn't much of a burden on either of us. Tim had a car he drove back and forth to work. Since I didn't have one, I relied on buses most of the time.

Tim felt pretty blue about breaking up with Mary. I didn't think he was at the time, but I'm sure he was seeing her, even though he had vowed never to again.

Our apartment was out quite a ways, and the last bus left the center of town about one in the morning. If you missed that one, you walked.

And so it was that I started walking home on a Sunday morning at 2 a.m. It was a clear, cold night and the stars glittered with a sharp, jagged light. A soft furry frost was beginning to cover everything, and my breath steamed around my head.

The streetlights began fading out as I got close to our neighborhood and darkness crowded up close all around. When your imagination works at that hour, you can see all kinds of creepy characters lurking among the shadows.

It was a much better night to be in than out, and I began trotting. I was looking forward to some hot coffee and I left the sidewalk for the middle of the street where I felt safer.

My fingers were numb from cold, and I fumbled around with the key before I got the door open. I switched the light on as I shoved it shut, and stopped dead in my tracks.

Everything was gone. The apartment had been cleaned out. Nothing we had moved in with was there: no coffee pot, no coffee, no blankets -- nothing. I thought we had been robbed.

Then I saw a note on the drainboard next to the sink. It was from Tim. I read it once, then glanced around the empty apartment. I was sure I had misread it, so I went back over it, slowly and carefully. But I hadn't.

He and Mary had decided to try it once more, he said. He apologized for the inconvenience he was causing me, but he hoped I would understand.

I didn't, but I do now -- I think. And I learned that the love bug can't be trusted. You never know how big a chunk it's taking out of you when it's biting someone else.

First Day On The Job
Can Be A Tough One

The first day on a new job is usually a little stressful. Occasionally, it can become a disaster, as my friend Mike discovered.

He found his first real job as a filling station attendant while he was still in high school, and he was elated. On his first day he showed up early.

He was quick and courteous. He smiled when customers drove in, and thanked them when they drove out. After a few hourse he was feeling pretty good about himself.

With a confident smile, he greeted a customer who was in a hurry. When he said, "Fill'er up," Mike quickly removed the cap on the gas tank and reached for the hose.

While the tank was filling he washed the windshield, checked the oil and made sure there was ample water in the battery. When the nozzle automatically shut off, he glanced at the total on the pump and told the man behind the wheel how much he owed. He handed Mike a credit card.

Mike hadn't filled out a receipt for a credit card, and it took him longer than he wanted it to. When he asked the driver to sign it, he apologized for being so slow.

But he was learning. And he decided the boss should be impressed by his performance as the car pulled away from the pump. Then he saw the nozzle sticking out of the car's gas tank.

When the car came to the end of the hose several things happened with unexpected suddenness.

First, the fender of the car developed some huge, unsightly wrinkles where the nozzle entered the tank. Then the nozzle broke, and the fitting on the pump wrenched around like a broken elbow.

Mike's dream of marching quickly up the ladder of success ended when the boss stepped out to see what had happened. He didn't have to be a reader of the Wall Street Journal to know that his career there had ended.

He was discouraged, to say the least. He wasn't quite as confident of

101

becoming chairman of Standard Oil's board of directors when he began looking for another job.

When he found one in another filling station he vowed that all nozzles would promptly be removed when the tank was full -- before the bill had been paid, while everything was still intact.

He was more cautious on his first day than he had been in his life. The smile he greeted customers with was tinged with business-like seriousness. He was doing OK.

Then a customer wheeled in off the street. But she didn't roll up and stop in front of the pumps the way most customers do. She sighted in on the nearest one and hit it head on while Mike stood open mouthed and watched.

This was more than a nozzle job, to be sure. Before her car bumped to a stop, it sheared the pump off at its base. A gassy smell quickly filled the air, just before the fumes blew up in a swoosh of flames.

The driver escaped, and so did Mike. But it turned into quite a spectacular morning before firemen arrived and doused the blaze. Not many filling stations provide that kind of excitement. I'm not sure many would want to.

Mike had nothing to do with the customer's erratic driving. But he was there when she clobbered the pump, and he began to feel that he was a jinx.

He hadn't intended to set the world on fire, he said. All he'd wanted was a job. The way things were going, he wondered if work was the right career for him.

That's the way it goes sometimes. The first day on a new job can determine a person's attitude for the rest of his life.

A couple of fellows I know had bad experiences during their first day on new jobs, and they decided work wasn't all it was cracked up to be -- and they never did it again. I don't think Mike can be blamed if he decides to follow suit.

Family Reunion Brings Bugs

It's the good old summertime, and time once more for picnics and family reunions. For variety, there's nothing like them.

I'm not sure why all the ants in the country decide to hold a picnic of their own when we do. And why they pick the same place -- at the same time -- is beyond me.

And never will I know why a swarm of yellowjackets insist on dropping in for a visit about the same time I get propped up against a tree with a plate full of fried chicken and all the trimmings balanced on one knee.

But they make for exciting dining. I recommend them highly to the Hilton and other fine eateries. They'll do wonders for business -- if there's any left.

Picnics also provide an ideal forum -- I think that's the term being widely used today -- for family reunions. They give you a chance to move around, to mingle freely with members of the clans.

Family reunions are important, I believe, because they give us an opportunity to glance up and down the family tree. They provide genealogical perspective.

You can see where you came from and by the looks of your progeny, you can let folks see what you're sending on down the line. It's sort of like putting the future on display.

I've always enjoyed the discreet comparisons families make between theirs and yours. In most cases, I've noticed, theirs comes off much better than yours -- if they're doing the talking. And vice versa, naturally.

Family reunions often become a contest in which parents attempt to make their children look better than anyone else's. And once they get the floor, they don't like to give it up.

Those doing the talking are convinced that what they have to say is more important than anything they will ever hear, and they are hard to dislodge.

"Oh, how nice," I heard one mother say as another talked glowingly of the manner in which her children were enriching the world. "We're so lucky the way things have turned out, aren't we?"

Notice the switch to "we," which gives the listener a subtle opportunity to break in with a few remarks that put anything the speaker said to shame.

And it's all done with good-natured nodding, and hand shaking and back patting because family reunions are designed to conceal envy while allowing it to be displayed in a frame of jovial restraint.

In fact, family reunions are miles of smiles laced with surreptitious speculation about what Martha has done to make her hair look so dark.

"Why, last time I saw her it was almost white!"

Although it was whispered, that exclamation was intended to be heard from one end of the table to the other -- and it was.

"And have you noticed how old Harry's looking? He sure has gained a lot of weight since..."

Most of us approach a family reunion like a buyer looking for a used car. We immediately look for flaws -- for signs of wear and tear.

But they're never alluded to. That's the unwritten law. After all the "Glad to see yous" have been spread around, it's time to get started on the "How well you looks."

Compliments come faster at a family reunion than promises at a political convention. Putting up with ants and yellowjackets is a minor aggravation when compared with all the nice things you'll hear said about yourself.

But don't take them seriously. Blood may be thicker than water, as it is written, but nothing is thinner than a compliment received at a family reunion. With one quick glance you can see clear through it.

Painstaking Look At Life

Brett was a moaner and a groaner. He always had something wrong with him. He complained continually.

He told anyone who would listen about his complaints. He loved to trap strangers who would sympathize with him, which was a mistake every stranger lived to regret.

It just made Brett hurt worse, it seemed. He could turn three words of sympathy into 15 minutes of complaint while warming up to the real issue, which was usually different on any given day.

I'm not sure how he chose his aches and pains. I thought for a while it had something to do with the moon, but I changed my mind. A full moon filled him with misery, but so did no moon at all.

Some days he seemed to hurt worse all over than anywhere else. At other times, the pain would localize in his arm or elbow. Sometimes it would settle in his toe or tibia.

He was tall and lean. He had a long, sad sallow face that looked like it had been copied out of some ancient medical journal. It was filled to overflowing with woe.

"I wonder why he puts up with himself," a fellow said to me one day. "You'd think he'd get sick to death after a while, which might not be too bad an idea."

He didn't. He just kept developing more aches and pains. It amazed me that one body could withstand so much torment, but it kept shuffling along.

And his wife kept shuffling along beside him. She was a small, tired-looking little woman who bore her burden in resigned silence. It was easy to see that he had complaints enough for both of them.

When Brett got together with another hypochondriac, misery piled upon misery. When they began discussing ailments, it was like listening to a talking medical dictionary, reduced to common everyday terms anyone could understand.

They could develop more specialized, localized pockets of pain than a computer could compute. During one short session they could take a barrel of pills. In 15 minutes, they could go through enough salves and ointments to stock a fair-sized hospital for a week or more.

But Brett usually won. He was one of the finest moaners and groaners I've ever seen. When it came to magnifying misery, he dwarfed all competitors.

Without taking a long breath, he could turn a simple cold into life-threatening pneumonia. When he put his mind to it, a blister could become a boil within minutes.

I met him while we were running an auction, which he attended every week. At first, I looked forward to his visits. You could never tell what new malady he would be contending with that day.

A lot of things can go wrong with the human body, but when you're going through three and four ailments a week, you may start repeating yourself. That's what happened to Brett. I guess all those aches and pains finally sapped his imagination.

I've often thought about the field day he could've had if television had been around then. In one evening he could have been exposed to more sinus congestion, more inflamed, painful-itching hemorrhoids, more decongested coughs and aggravated jock itch than he could have dreamed of.

I'm sure it would have done wonders for his repertoire. And I can imagine how good it would have made him feel.

The Sad End Of Happiness

Leon was an admirable kid. He was always cheerful, and he seemed to have a sense of purpose. He didn't have time for adolescent instability. He had too much to do.

When I met him he was about 13, dark-haired with blue eyes and the whitest teeth you've ever seen. He was a good looking kid. And he had what seemed to me an exciting background.

He was from the Midwest -- North or South Dakota, I believe. But his parents were separated, and he had lived with his mother until she could no longer support him and the rest of the kids. That was in the late 1930s, long before the government got into the business of welfare on a bloated scale.

So Leon left home. He rode freight trains west to Oregon, where his uncle lived. To hear him describe it, it was some trip. Not a very pleasant one, either. I remember him telling how hungry he would get. Since he was too proud to beg, he was hungry most of the way. A couple of times, he said, older hobos buddy up to him, but usually for the wrong reasons. So he remained a loner.

When he finally made it to Oregon, his uncle found him a job on a ranch, where he worked for room and board while going to high school. It was no gravy train. He got up early to do chores before he left for school, and he left as soon as school was out to do chores in the evening.

But he seemed happy, and he was well liked. He enjoyed sports, and he played with enthusiasm. I'm sure he would have made the basketball team if he could have stayed after school to practice.

He was an optimist, and I'm sure he looked forward to a rosy future. Then World War II came along and tore up all our lives, and I lost track of him. I thought about him, though, and wondered how he was doing.

With his attitude I knew he would make it all right. And I figured that those beautiful white teeth would shine through a smile regardless of how tough it got.

Time passed. A lot of time. And I remember how surprised I was one

107

afternoon when the phone rang and Leon was on the other end. He was passing through, he said, and wondered if he could come out for a while that evening. "Sure," I said. "Come on out and spend the night."

He hadn't changed much. He was still good looking. His hair was still dark and he looked almost as young as he had when we were going to school. Time had let him off pretty easy.

But something was different. The smile wasn't there anymore, and he didn't laugh the way I remembered him laughing. There was something melancholy about his smile when it did come on, and there was a sadness in his eyes that I hadn't expected to see.

No, he said, he had never married. And no, he didn't suppose he ever would. And no, he didn't find much pleasure in the work he was doing, and no, no, no -- to everything.

With him he had a guitar and after a while he wondered if we would like to hear him sing some songs he had written. They, too, were tinged with sadness, and a melancholy somberness. And one theme kept recurring: those rootless years as an adolescent, those years when he was on his own.

It's strange. At least it appears strange to me. The very circumstances that I thought would have made him equal to any situation were the ones that had blighted his life.

Instead of taking pride in his resourcefulness as a kid -- instead of being proud of the courage it had taken to do the things he did -- he was bitter and resentful because he hadn't had a home and family.

Some lives, it seems, are governed by an irony hard to comprehend.

Fortune Teller Almost Palms
A Five-Spot

Her eyes were big and brown, deep and mysterious. They were filled with the wisdom of the ages, or so it seemed. She smiled when I sat down.

For $5, she said, she would read the palm of one hand. For $10, she would read both of my palms. For $25, she promised to reveal my entire future by combining what she had already been paid $10 to see.

I handed her a $10 bill and told her I wanted one palm read. She reached for the money, then my left hand. She held it firmly. She held the $10 even more firmly.

When I reminded her that I was to get $5 back, she nodded. "Not to worry," she said. Her smile was warm and reassuring.

But it slowly faded when she bent over my palm. I thought of a cloud crossing in front of the sun as I watched a frown cover her face. Something did not bode well for me, it seemed.

One thing I could depend on, she said: I would live a long time. It was very obvious. From the look on her face, I wasn't sure I wanted to.

"The life line is so long and strong," she said, it would stand much erosion before it disappeared with me.

If that was consolation, the grip she had on my $10 was not. I gave it an anxious glance, and she patted my hand affectionately.

Whle she was telling me about the long life I was going to lead, the frown on her face disappeared. But an expression of profound sadness replaced it when she looked again into my palm. Obviously, my hand was a map of misery.

It appeared, she said, that the life I had led -- and the long life I would lead -- had been -- and would be -- at times tumultuous, sometimes, she opined, it might appear to be on the brink of disaster.

Her eyes filled with pity at the thought. An unfinished chapter from the Book of Job couldn't have read worse than I was beginning to feel.

"You put up a good front," she told me, "but it is not your true self. You are deeply troubled. Is that right?"

My eyes strayed to the $10 bill. "Not to worry," she said, as she shook her head. "It's in good hands." She didn't crack a smile. I didn't either. It was serious business.

Perhaps she is deliberately dooming me with my left hand, I thought, so she can save me with my right one -- for another $5, of course. If she hadn't miscalculated, she would have pulled it off, because I was getting desperate for some good news.

Instead of sinking me deeper into despair, she offered me a sliver of hope. She had to search quite a while before she found it hiding in a crease at the base of my thumb.

Thursday and Friday would be good luck for me, she said. Very lucky days, indeed. She wouldn't tell me what form the luck was going to take. She wanted it to be a surprise.

On that uplifting note I decided to leave. When I stood, her eyes filled with reproach. "I have more to tell," she said. When I shook my head, her hand started going very slowly into her blouse for the $5 I had coming. Very slowly, indeed.

To make sure my luck had ample opportunity to do its stuff, I bought five lottery tickets. I was as smug as the guy who buys a life insurance policy two days before he passes on. For once I figured I had outsmarted the system.

After I tossed the lottery tickets into the trash on Thursday, I decided Friday would be my lucky day. It wasn't. Not unless you call a flat tire a pleasant surprise.

It didn't augur well for me. In fact, it seemed to fulfill the fortune teller's doleful prognostication. I couldn't remember her getting enthusiastic about the good things coming my way, but she had waxed most eloquently about the dark side of my future.

An unsettling realization, to be sure. I'm beginning to wonder if my left hand is friend or foe. It almost makes me want to shorten my life line.

Tourists Often Blind
Themselves To Reality

The old lady sat on a dirty sidewalk beside a small tin cup in a Mexican border town. She was blind and she was begging.

But she didn't ask for money. She didn't plead. She didn't even move. She sat so still she could have been a carving.

Border towns are tourist traps, where Americans swarm like bees. They go to see the sights, to haggle with the shopkeepers and buy a bottle of cheap tequila.

To the old lady's silent plea, most tourists were indifferent. They swept on the way they would have passed a tire blown out on the highway. They looked, then looked away, because that which cannot be seen doesn't exist if it can be forgotten.

I heard one tourist say she was being used for bait. In a loud, clear voice that could be heard for a block, he told the fellow with him that her family had put her there to wring money out of gullible, sympathetic Americans.

"She can see as well as you and I can," he said.

If she was a pathetic figure in a harmless scam, it wasn't very profitable. Late in the afternoon, a few small coins failed to cover the bottom of the cup. If she could have seen, I don't think she would have consented to sit still all day for such a pittance.

So many anguished eyes have beseeched us from flickering TV screens we have become shockproof. So many people with wasted limbs have been exploited by governments who ask for aid that is not delivered, we've become blase.

Misery in such measure blunts out senses, and I probably could have forgotten that old lady. But there is something poignant and compelling about silent appeals.

They stick longer in the mind than the pleading of those who walk and talk and see. They are easier to brush aside because they arouse our suspicions and we are not plagued by guilt when we say, "No."

111

In a deep pool of silent thought the old lady passed her days. She had submerged into another world -- a mute world of her own. In a sea of chaotic sound she had withdrawn to some secret place.

She was wizened and small, so dry and juiceless her face looked like an orange that had puckered in the sun. I wondered when it had last brightened with a smile? How long since laughter had paid a visit?

And what did she see in the darkened closets of her mind? Were they filled with memories bright as a tight red sash? And skirts that unfurled like flags in a dance of youthful abandon?

When the present comes up tight against a future that is running out, the mind becomes a theater and memory entertains with re-runs from the past. Then those special moments that bloomed like flowers along the way come back to life again.

For a frame or two they warm the blood and revive desires curled up in hibernation. For a frame or two the music comes again and the moon wraps a promise in a misty, golden light.

In her secret place, I hope the blind old lady was treated to some special moments. She looked like she deserved it.

I don't think there had been many in her life. She looked too tired and weary. I have a feeling that her theater closed early, a casualty of work and worry.

When I think about her, I see tattered posters peeling off sunbaked walls -- old advertisements for happy double features she never got to see.

A Look At Life From Two Directions

Once I took a job building an addition on a beach cottage. It was during the summer and it was nice on the coast. Some mornings it was like driving into a different world. It would be sunny and bright a few miles inland, but along the coast it would be cool and foggy. The abruptness of the change always surprised me.

I had quite a lot of company on that job. Living across the road was an old man, who had retired years before. Nearly every day he would come over to see how I was doing. And he always came with the latest fishing report, because that's what he did the most of. Occasionally, he would bring a fish over late in the afternoon so it wouldn't spoil before I got it home.

He had a dog. He called him Skipper. He was a black and white spaniel. I envied him. He was always so sleek and well groomed. For a long time I didn't think he had a worry in the world.

But one afternoon he came over and sniffed all around, then went back across the road to the trailer house where he and the old man lived. In a little while he was back. I don't know how many times he made that trip during the afternoon, but a few more times and he would have grooved out a permanent trail. He was a worried dog.

When he came back from fishing, Skipper and the old man had a touching reunion. It seemed that Skipper had gadded off somewhere, and the old man hadn't been able to find him when he got ready to go. He wouldn't have gone at all, he said, but he had another fellow waiting for him. He hadn't caught any fish, and he supposed it was because he was worried about Skipper and couldn't keep his mind on his business.

He scolded Skipper in a soft voice that didn't have much sting in it, and Skipper crowded up close against his leg. The shine that the old man's absence had wiped out of his eyes was back, and his little stub of a tail was standing proudly erect as they walked slowly up the hill to the trailer house. As I watched them, I couldn't help but think that worry is sometimes worth the relief that comes when it ends.

113

Next door to the house I was working on there lived a fellow who had been a merchant sailor. He had been in every deepwater port in the world. From the way he talked, I assumed that he had visited every bar in every one of them. He was living on a disability pension. His back had never recovered from a fall he had taken.

His 50th birthday was coming up. He wanted to make it a memorable occasion, and he jumped off to an early start. Whle he was carousing around the bars downtown I didn't see him. When his money started running low, he began tapering off at home. His brand of booze got cheaper, and once in a while he would step out on his porch to see if the world was still there.

On the morning of his 50th birthday he yelled at me as I was unloading tools. He wanted me to come over. As I sat down at the kitchen table he poured me a cup of coffee with a shaky hand and gave himself a refill. He didn't look very happy, but I wished him a happy birthday all the same.

As he took a chair across from me, he sadly shook his head. ''By God, I'll tell you one thing,'' he said. ''I sure feel like I'm 50 years old today.''

What a contrast they were. The old man talked about things he and Skipper were going to do, while Mort talked about the things he had done. For the old man and Skipper each day was a new beginning. For Mort it was 24 hours of endlessness.

Life is certainly a point of view. When you see it from the wrong end things look mighty cockeyed. And pretty dark and dismal when you open your eyes one morning and discover that you've drowned more than half of it in a bottle of booze.

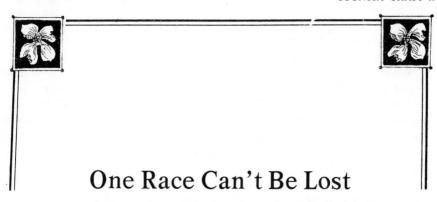

One Race Can't Be Lost

It was a lonesome place in Nevada. From a distance it looked like a mirage floating in a rolling, wind-whipped sea of desert brown. As I drove closer the buildings began to define themselves.

Not with pride, however, nor long, clean graceful lines. They slouched along the narrow highway that came curling down off the hill and sped on by in a straight line like a thread rushing into the distance.

I pulled into the only gas station there. An awning extended out from the office to cover two old pumps with loose, slack hoses draped around them like a pair of sickly snakes.

Out of the garage attached to the office a boy came pushing a bicycle. He was probably 10 or 11. He was a skinny little guy, with a mop of loose brown hair and wary blue eyes.

When I asked him if he was in charge, he shook his head. His dad had walked down to the store, he told me, and he would be back in a little bit.

It irritated me a little to think that anyone running a business would walk off in the middle of the day without regard for customers who had more important things to do with their time.

But I waited because that was the only service station within 70 or 80 miles, and I needed gas. As I got out of the car and stretched, the boy rolled his bike a few feet closer.

"This is a good old bicycle," he said.

I told him it looked like it.

But it didn't. It was an oldtimer, a relic. The fenders were gone and the tires were smooth. The only redeeming features were the handlebars. They were turned down in a way that gave it a reckless, rakish appearance.

"It's fast," he said. As he laid his hand on the black, worn seat he glanced shyly at me out of the corner of his eye.

"A real speedster, huh?"

He smiled to himself, the way one does who sees a memory that pleases him. "Sometimes it goes too fast," he said softly.

115

"Does it run away with you?"

"Sometimes I can't hold it back."

"It must have a mind of its own."

When he saw that I wasn't making fun of him, his eyes brightened and he began talking. The words tumbled out as his imagination took over.

A day or two before, he said, he had been riding on the shoulder of the highway and it had taken off. "I tried to hold it back," he said, "but I couldn't. All I could do was hang on and it kept going faster and faster..."

"That's enough," said the lean, dried-out fellow in bib overalls who came around the corner of the station.

The bright-eyed, excited eagerness in the boy's face went out like a light as he flipped the switch on his imagination, where he was happiest.

"Marvin gets a little carried away at times," his dad said, as he squinted against the sun. Marvin shot me a defeated glance as he went around the corner.

He was riding along the side of the highway when I left. I'm sure he was there so he could wave as I went by. I watched in the rear view mirror as he leaned low over the handlebars and started pumping hard.

In his mind he had already passed me. I was eating his dust because those were races he never lost. I'm glad he won them because he became a loser every time his dad spoke to him.

Paper Sack Holds More Than Its Contents

On a cold, blustery day about a year ago, I saw a fellow hunched up beside the road as he tried to protect a paper sack from the wind and rain.

He raised his thumb as I approached and I pulled over. Whatever he was trying to keep dry was going to get wet unless I gave him a ride.

He thanked me for the lift as he crawled in. When he opened the sack to see if the package inside was dry I saw a swatch of red-green wrapping paper.

He was hitchhiking from Medford, he told me, and he was headed for a small town on the coast. He lived there with his wife and daughter, or had until the sawmill where he'd worked shut down.

He had gone to Medford to work in the fruit harvest. When it ended he found a job in a warehouse, where pears were stored before they were shipped. But it had ended and he was out of work again.

It hadn't paid much, but he was willing to take anything. His unemployment had run out, he said, and he was scraping the bottom of the barrel.

He leaned back in the seat and shoved his black baseball cap up. He rubbed his eyes. He hadn't been near a razor for two or three days, and he needed a haircut. He was tired. He had been hitchhiking all night, without much luck.

"Not much moving this time of year," he said. "A few trucks is about all, and they won't stop because they aren't supposed to pick anyone up."

When I glanced at the sack, he told me it was a present for his daughter. He and his wife had agreed not to get each other anything because they were so tight financially.

"But I want her to have a Christmas," he said.

He had bought her a doll. He smiled when he told me that. Then he spent a long time staring out the window at the rain.

"How old is your daughter?"

"Four," he said.

117

"She'll like that doll."

"It's not as fancy as the one I wanted to get her," he said.

"She won't know the difference," I told him. "She'll think it's the finest doll in the world."

"But I'll know," he said, "and that makes a difference to me."

He wasn't used to being destitute. He had made good money until the lumber market had gone to pot. Now, he said, he couldn't even pay his bills.

His wife had taken a job as a waitress. He didn't object to that, not if that was what she wanted to do. But she had taken one because she had to, and that had hurt his pride. He felt like he had let his family down.

He shook his head and rubbed his hands together the way a man does who wants to get a hold on something -- something solid and substantial. Then he reached down and twisted the top of the sack tight around the package.

"Long as Laura's happy," he said. "That's all that counts right now."

It was drizzling when I let him out. And I watched him head down the road with the package bulging under his coat.

I hadn't realized until then how much love a wrinkled paper sack could hold.

The Flavor Of Life

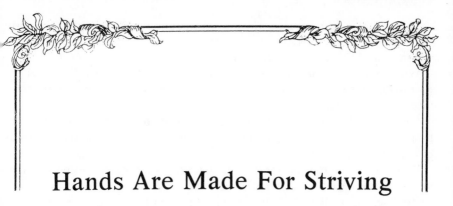

Hands Are Made For Striving

I was lying flat on my back beneath a pickup. With my fingers I was trying to take out a bolt that I couldn't reach with a wrench, and dirt was an avalanche falling in my face.

That isn't a predicament that usually produces great insight, but suddenly I became aware of something I had taken for granted: the agility of the human hand.

I shouldn't have been surprised. Long before I reached for that bolt my hands had been doing what I wanted them to. But I had failed to appreciate their capabilities.

I flexed my fingers. Then I held them off to one side so I could see their silhouette in the light that was seeping under the pickup.

Instantly, without benefit of switches or relays, they obeyed my commands. No computer was needed. No wires had to be strung. No buttons had to be pushed.

As I glanced at the underside of the pickup, I realized that everything there had been done by someone's hands. All the bolts and gears, the frame and braces, the transmission and differential -- everything was the result of someone's handiwork.

Life is a miracle that excites my awe and wonder. Even the simplest is complex beyond comprehension. The eyes and ears are nothing short of phenomenal, and the hands we use are in a class all by themselves.

They reach for the brush that paints the masterpiece. They hold the pencil that writes the symphony and guide the pen that writes the poem. With inspired fingers was the Bible written.

Skyscrapers stand because of many hands. Without them, there wouldn't be any majestic bridges, any great ships or trembling trestles crossed by rumbling locomotives.

What would we do for roads if there were no hands to build them? How would we steer our cars? How would we eat that bowl of soup if we couldn't hold the spoon?

I haven't the slightest idea why we were put on Earth. Sometimes I think the Creator was dissatisfied with what He had done and wanted it destroyed. Given time, I think we may succeed.

With hands that must have tingled with strange excitement, Eve reached for the forbidden fruit and plunged us into centuries of despair with one tiny bite. Or so the story goes.

Since then, I thought, as I lay beneath the pickup on the damp and chilly ground, we have been reaching for the latch to a door we cannot find. What a quandary, what an enigma life is.

While one hand reaches for the pen to write an eulogy for those who died in some insane conflict, another is signing a nation to war. While this hand writes the poem, that hand slashes with the sword.

There are hands that destroy, and hands that soothe. Hands that help, and hands that harm. And the mystery is compounded because the helping hand today may be the hand that hurts tomorrow.

Hand over hand, I thought, as I crawled out from under the pickup, we make our way along the thread of life. And when we climb, we're always in danger of falling back.

Occasionally our grip is so sure and confident we swing and soar up high where the sun is bright and the sky is blue. And when we think we are safe and secure our grip falls and we begin to slip.

But all's not lost, because hands are made for striving. And they are in no position to swing a sword when they are reaching for a sun that's brighter and a sky that's bluer.

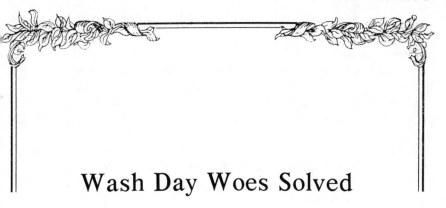

Wash Day Woes Solved

Clotheslines were one of the most neglected necessities on a farm or ranch. Where they haven't been replaced by a clothes dryer, they are still.

Any old pole stuck in the ground with a wire strung between it and another one slanting off toward the North Pole was considered good enough by those who put them up.

I guess that's understandable. They were usually put up by men for women to use, which is a bit different than putting them up for their own use. They were never considered as important as a hinge on a barn door.

Most clothesline poles were outcasts before they were ever put up. You could tell by the way they slouched that they had inferiority complexes. Most of them had some pretty knotty problems.

To brace them, baling wire wrapped around the top of the posts would be anchored to stakes driven into the ground at either end. That was usually an emergency measure, intended to prolong their misery until another batch of clothes could be dried.

If no baling wire was around, anything would do. I've seen twine used, and old ropes. Anything that would give posts the illusion that they were being supported was considered sufficient.

Usually it wasn't, but those poor old posts had pride. They wouldn't keel over without reason. They usually waited until the lines were loaded with clothes, so they would have a good excuse for going down.

That invariably aroused some rather strong emotions among women who had spent half a day washing clothes on a washboard -- or an old wringer washer. The men who had cobbled up the clotheslines were lucky if they were off in the fields somewhere. They were smart if they stayed there until sometime the next day -- or the day after that.

Women had sufficient reason for losing their tempers. Nine times out of ten there was no grass under the lines and all the clothes they had scrubbed so hard came to rest in dry powdery dust that tinged them dark brown like molasses.

There was nothing to do, of course, but do it all over again. Many a frustrated tear has been shed over a collapsed clothesline, and justifiably so. If the feminist movement didn't begin with one, I'll be surprised.

But even worse than weak clothesline poles were weaker fences. Especially on wash day because cattle that get out love to investigate things hanging from a line.

If it happened to be a hot day they soon discovered that all those damp, cool clothes were ideal for brushing flies off their backs. You could tell they really appreciated such amenities by the way they took refuge among the nightshirts and the nighties.

But the fun began when bulls decided they saw an imaginary enemy hanging on the line. With a stiff legged charge they would attack a pillow case, or a billowing white sheet. You can imagine what happened when they got tangled up in something and decided it was time to leave.

I once saw a bull take off after he had snagged a pair of overalls with his horns. When the pole broke he got tangled up in the clothesline, which added haste to his departure. The line followed him, of course, and so did the clothes.

He looked like a ship flying flags from a dozen different nations as he sailed around the corner of the house. Magellan would have been proud of him, but the lady of the house wasn't. She just about torpedoed him with a skillet as he sped by.

I thought for a long time that the problem with clothes lines was without solution, but I am mistaken. I came to that conclusion the other day when I drove by a farm where the wash had been hung out to dry on fences around the house.

It looked like it had been hung artistically over holes in the fence so the cattle could find their way out. Since nothing was flopping from a line, they weren't interested enough to ever investigate.

Everything looked so peaceful and serene I couldn't believe it was wash day. I was used to excitement: to anger -- to passionate outbursts that flamed as bright as the red drawers hanging on the gate.

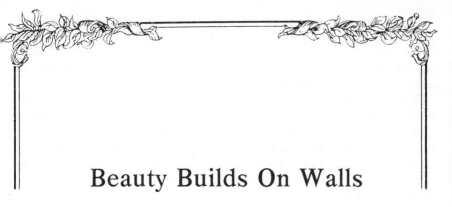

Beauty Builds On Walls

In the barn there is a piece of lumber I'm saving. It is a thing of beauty.

It isn't large. It's only 1 inch thick and 2 feet long. But it is 20 inches wide, without seam or joint, which makes it unique in my opinion.

The grain is tight from years of growing slowly, and there is not a blemish on it. It was cut from a log when Northwest mills were sawing old-growth timber that measured 4, 5, and 6 feet in diameter.

I believe it has done its duty. It was once a shelf in a 100-year-old house we remodeled. I've retired it to the corner of the barn. I'm protecting it for posterity.

From that same house I also saved a stack of rough 1x12's that were used for the interior walls. They bear the scars of saws that cut them years and years ago. They are still covered with the tacks that held the muslin that the wallpaper was pasted to.

I'm not going to retire them. They were not made for show. They don't have the personality of that wide, fine-grained specimen. If they were horses, it would be a thoroughbred, and the 1x12's would be Mustangs, tough and hard to break.

I compared them recently while wainscoting a room with pine, 3 inches wide. It too, was a thoroughbred. It was clean and smooth. It smelled good.

Every effort will be made to beautify it. It will be painted, pampered and preserved. It will lead a life of ease.

As it ages, it will darken into a lustrous hue. It will be praised and admired. It will remain sheltered, warm and dry.

Beauty has privilege, no doubt about it. The wide, broad board I'm saving is well protected. The 1x12's are not so lucky. If the wind blows hard while it is raining, they may get soaked.

Lucky are the things with which we decorate our lives. They know not what hardship is.

Aesthetics do strange things to our perceptions, it seems to me. When

123

they warp our logic and skew our vision, we tend to overlook the source of things.

Who gives thought to the ore that nurtured the diamond's brilliant flash and set the ruby aflame? Who knows what happened to the oyster that dressed the grain of sand in milky white?

They fade quickly into oblivion. Like the shuck that protects the golden ear of corn, they are cast aside. They hear the chill wind of indifference blow.

As I carefully put a clean, white piece of pine in place, I thought: This is not really the wall, but with its beauty, it will deceive one into thinking so.

The studs should get the credit since they provide the support, but no one thinks of them. They remain forever anonymous because they aren't pretty enough to be exposed.

The sheathing that covers them was put on diagonally to give the wall its strength. It is seamed with pitch in places, and here and there a knot fell out.

It, too, is an ugly duckling that won't be seen. In obscurity it draws tight around the nails that hold it. Sometimes when it strains against a heavy wind, it can be heard to creak.

Softly, however, because it is muffled by the cedar siding that was precisely cut to conceal it. No hammer hit it hard enough to leave a mark because it was what the world would see.

The studs became the backbone on which illusions have been hung. Without it -- without backbone -- we would soon run out of illusions.

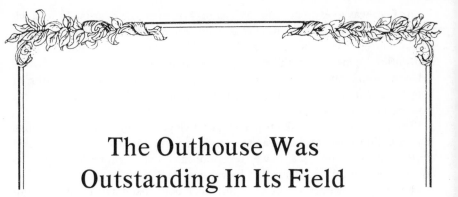

The Outhouse Was Outstanding In Its Field

Outhouses are not supposed to be models of architectural excellence. No World's Fair that I know of ever exhibited one as an outstanding example of pipeless plumbing.

But I know one that should have been. It was the handiwork of my brother Buggs and me. It was probably the far-outest house that was ever built.

Actually, I misrepresent the facts when I say we built it. That gives the impression that we adhered to a prearranged plan, a blueprint of sorts. We didn't.

The plan simply evolved as we went along. It didn't have any more idea where it was going than we did. I think it just tagged along out of curiosity to see what shape it was going to take.

I'm not a builder. When I cut a board to fit, it usually doesn't. When I cut a 45-degree angle, it looks like a horseshoe after a long hard ride.

However, I can drive nails. I've had a lot of experience. If all the nails I've bent while trying to drive them were joined, they would encircle Dolly Parton at her epicenter.

I'm not much of a craftsman, but I like to have things look halfway presentable when I'm through. In comparison to Buggs, I'm a perfectionist.

He doesn't waste time worrying about such frivolous things as appearance. Since he doesn't expect a board he cuts to fit, he doesn't fiddle around with careful measurements. He doesn't worry about foregone conclusions.

I realize now that he had the right idea. We didn't have much to work with, so he didn't see any reason to make something look nice that didn't care how it looked anyway.

Outhouses don't seem to. It's probably a trait they inherited. It's the result, I think, of genetic indifference. Since they were usually stuck way out behind, they naturally developed a dark, drab complex.

Buggs and I didn't disappoint the image outhouses have of themselves when we erected ours. The best we did looked as if it had been worked over by a wrecking crew before we were through.

The floor was uneven because we couldn't find enough boards of the same thickness. But we laid them so that a person who tripped while entering would fall forward rather than backward. We thought that would be more appropriate, considering the nature of the building.

I don't remember what we used for studs, but they were of different lengths. The longest ones were none too long, and the shortest ones were far from being long enough.

We covered the roof with tar paper, but it sloped off in so many directions that rain didn't know which way to run. So it seeped in under the paper and dripped all over the seat. A wet reception awaited the tortured soul who couldn't wait until the storm had blown over.

The sides we covered with tin that had been used twice before. Sun shining through the old nail holes cast designs upon the floor that I saw later entitled modern art. Buggs and I were way ahead of our time and didn't know it.

It was customary then for Halloween pranksters to tip outhouses over, but they never touched that one. The reason was obvious. It was built along such uncertain lines that no one knew which way it would fall.

But it wasn't happy. I don't think it liked being ignored. Its tar paper roof curled up in a frown, and depression was evident in the swing of its door. One day it collapsed on its own.

Being different, I guess, was more painful than being overturned as a member of the crowd.

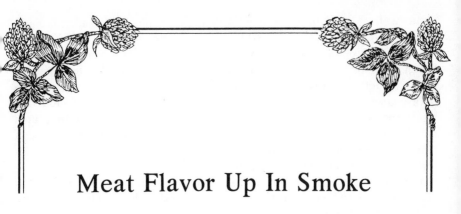

Meat Flavor Up In Smoke

We used to smoke our bacon and hams in a tall, narrow, stovepipe-looking building that acquired a dark brown, well-seasoned appearance over the years.

After the meat had been soaked in a thick briney solution it was hung in the smokehouse over a small, smoldering smudge of a fire, because green wood was the kind to use. It was smoke we wanted, not flame.

It seems that everyone had their favorite wood, which gave the meat a distinctive flavor as it absorbed the rich smokey aroma. If I remember right, we used green apple wood.

Occasionally, a ham or bacon would have a tart, tangy taste like it had been exposed to the smoke of a crab apple tree. But it was nothing to worry about. Dad said that sometimes happened when we didn't "get a good scald on things."

Once in a while one would get an awful yen for salt, which it would absorb while in the brine. If you took a bit of it you would think that you had forked up the salt shaker by mistake.

As you grabbed for the milk -- or coffee so hot it would sear the taste buds off your tongue -- or anything that looked like liquid -- you would wonder why it wasn't in the Great Salt Lake where it belonged.

But those were exceptions. Most of the time the taste of home-cured ham and bacon couldn't be beat. And on a cold wintry morning they were a real delight because they gave you something to concentrate on besides the nasty weather that had hung the eaves with icicles sharp as daggers. Just thinking about it makes me want to fork up another slab of ham.

But time marches on and things pass away, as did those ancient smokehouses that looked like leaky old corncob pipes with wisps of smoke curling lazily out through the cracks. When they went, so did those rich tantalizing tastes. And I suppose the old apple tree watched them go with a sigh of relief.

But we lost something when smokehouses disappeared. And it is more elemental than taste alone. I would rather go to Reno -- much rather, in fact -- and take my chances on a slot machine than buy a package of supermarket bacon and expect to find a slice that will only be half as small after it is fried as it was before you laid it out cold and flabby in the skillet.

Of course, each package of bacon is designed with a small window that lets consumers see what they are buying. And the people who design them should be commended. They've raised the art of illusion to heights of disillusionment that couldn't have been imagined. They can show you things that aren't there and make you believe it.

What looks through the window like rigorous, healthy slices of bacon that came from hogs who took pride in their accomplishments, comes out as limp as a New Year's resolution on the first day of February.

And when it gets near the skillet it begins to curl up with embarrassment, which it should. For promising so much, and producing so little, it should suffer shame.

And how, I wonder, can they slice it so thin that two-ply toilet tissue feels like cardboard in comparison?

I'm surprised magicians haven't spotted the potential in modern-type bacon. It would be a natural for them. All they'd have to do is wave it over a warm skillet and it would vanish: "Now you see it, folks, and now you don't."

Where, you ask, did it go?

Straight into someone's profit margin, I suppose. But not yours. You'll have to be content with an empty skillet, and the vague feeling that you saw it just before it shriveled up and disappeared.

Pliers Pull Through The Years

My dad didn't give a hoot for tools. He figured he could fix anything that needed fixing with a screwdriver and a pair of pliers.

If it was a really big job, such as a major engine overhaul, he might use a hammer to knock things into place if profanity didn't do the job. As a result, he had the best used hammers around.

I guess I should have said hammer heads, because a broken handle seldom got replaced. Anyone who has tried to force a handle into an old hammer knows it is easier to buy a used one at an auction.

Nothing short of nitroglycerin would have blown the broken handles out of the hammer heads I've worked on. To simplify matters, we sometimes threw them into the stove and let the splintery ends burn out.

That was the easiest. The heat sometimes took the temper out of the hammer and it would get soft as modeling clay, which was fine -- if you were driving rubber nails.

But Dad had one unfailing ally in his mechanical arsenal: baling wire. Anything that couldn't be bolted, brazed, hammered or soldered back together got itself wired up.

I guess that's the reason he wasn't concerned about having a chest full of tools. With baling wire waiting at every bend, he considered tools a waste of money.

As indifferent as he was to most tools, he was deeply attached to a pair of fencing pliers that his dad had used. For them he had real feeling.

They were old. He said they were second-hand when Granddad got them. If you've done any fencing you know the kind of pliers I'm talking about. They are designed to do most anything that can be done with wire.

They are a hammer, fence stretcher and wire cutter all in one. They are equipped with a spur that can be driven under staples that need to be pulled. With wire pliers it wouldn't take more than a month or two to fence in all of New Mexico.

Dad discarded a hundred handle-less hammers. He broke dozens of plain pliers and bent untold screwdrivers. He even lost a couple of pretty good wrenches he had splurged on, but he never lost those old fencing pliers.

I remember the way the handles stuck up in the rear pocket of Granddad's overalls when he "commenced to fixing fence." And I remember the contented way they lay in his hand because they knew each other well.

When he fished them out of his pocket they performed miracles. Fences that were sick and saggy stood up a little straighter when he and those pliers went to work on them.

Fences never really looked healthy when he got through because he didn't consider fence building an art. But they always looked as if they would stand until the undertaker arrived.

When Granddad left us, his pliers passed on to Dad. And they remained as capable as ever. The two of them could stretch a mile of droopy barbed wire with just a little help now and then from a strand or two of baling wire.

After Dad died they became mine, and I took better care of them than he or Granddad ever had. I even oiled them a couple of times. I expected them to last forever, but they disappointed me.

Not long ago, while I was driving the spur under a staple I was trying to pry out of a gate post, they broke. The spur snapped off, along with one of the jaws.

As I pieced them together on the ground, I could see them bobbing peacefully along in Granddad's baggy pocket. And I watched once more the wonders they worked in Dad's hands. With the old masters gone, I guess they just didn't want to settle for anything less.

Experts will tell you that metal fatigue did them in, but I disagree. I think they died of a broken heart. That's the way it felt to me, anyway.

Beware Of The Settling Sawdust

It was an old building -- an old pump house that had been insulated with sawdust. It had been built upon big rocks spaced five feet apart, but they had settled and the building had come to rest upon the ground. When moisture began seeping up into the walls they began to rot.

It had been a good, solid well-built building, but it had tipped so badly on one end it appeared in danger of falling on its face before we got around to fixing it. At first we thought about tearing it down, but after we had checked a second time we changed our minds. By jacking it up and pouring a solid concrete foundation we thought it could be saved.

The sawdust was old and mouldy and musty so we decided to replace it with commercial insulation, which won't rot if it gets a little wet. The ceiling was so low a person of average height couldn't stand straight, and there were no windows, which made it dark inside. To clear the sawdust out of the walls we decided to strip the siding off the outside so we could see what we were doing.

Apparently the walls had been put up and a hole 2½ inches in diameter had been bored in the top plate between every two studs. The sawdust was then poured into the hole to fill the cavity. When the building was new I suppose the sawdust completely filled the space between the studs.

For mice it was an ideal home. It was warm in the sawdust, and dry. It was not an easy place to get to, which protected them from predators. But there was a flaw in their paradise. As the bottom of the wall rotted away, the sawdust gradually settled.

Imperceptibly, the distance between the sawdust and the hole increased, but the increase was so slight it didn't alarm the inhabitants. They didn't realize they were living in a trap.

Inevitably came the day when the distance between the sawdust and the hole became too great to jump, and there was no escape. What a frenzy must have followed. Lying on the sawdust between the studs we found their tiny skeletons, more fragile and delicate than the daintiest drawings. And

131

they remained intact. By some remaining bit of tendon they were held together.

At first I thought they had been trapped after falling through the holes, but they had lived there. Their nests remained, and scattered about were skeletons of all sizes. The finest home they could have found had become their grave. Is there a crueler form of irony?

One discovery we made was more startling than the others. Between two studs we found a skunk huddled up in the sawdust. It looked bigger than the hole, but that was the only way it could have gotten there. It was probably exploring when it wriggled through the hole and dropped in between the studs. By then the sawdust had settled so far the hole was out of reach.

It was completely mummified. The temperature and humidity had combined to preserve it completely. Its pelt was still in good shape. Even the odor was in good shape. It looked as though it were sleeping as it leaned against the wall with its nose resting between its front feet. There was no telling how many years it had been there, but it had been awhile. The outline of its body was smudged upon the board it had leaned against so long.

It seems a cruel and senseless way for anything to die. But who knows, if there is a purpose in the Grand Plan, then such things have their place. Every time I pass that old pump house now I wonder if there is anyone among us who has not felt the sawdust settle ever so slightly beneath his feet.

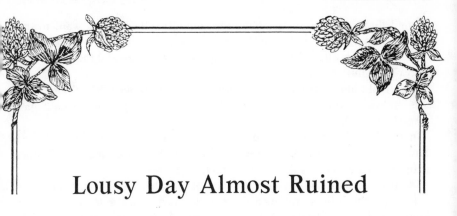

Lousy Day Almost Ruined

I never dug a posthole I really liked. I might have changed my mind if just once I'd dug one that opened up a gold mine, or an oil well in Iran, instead of blisters on my hands.

They're all bad, but some are worse than others. And the worst of all are those that have to be dug where a post has broken off. Digging the splintery end out of a hole that no longer exists is slower than eating spaghetti with a spear.

And that's the way it was going a couple of weeks ago as I sweated over a gate post that had been snapped off at ground level by an errant tractor.

The first fall rains had softened the ground, but not much. I should have waited. Since then enough moisture has fallen to float it out of the ground -- with the hole still attached.

However, dry ground wasn't the only problem. The gate is next to the highway and I had snitched some rocks off the shoulder of the road to tamp around the post when I put it in the first time.

I soon discovered something everyone who's done any fencing discovers: it is a lot easier to tamp a rock in than it is to untamp it. And since that part of the post that's broken off prevents you from digging out the old hole, you've got to dig a new one down through the rocks next to it so you've got room to pry what's left of the old one out. As you can see, it gets complicated.

Dark-brown thoughts were beginning to fester in my mind as I slaved away. Then I heard voices. I straightened up and listened. Were they coming from the hole? They sounded like it, and I thought: For once you've gone too far.

But they weren't. They were coming from two small boys walking along the highway. One had a sack swung over his shoulder. They were picking up cans and bottles.

They were about nine or ten, I imagine. They were happy, good looking boys and they stopped for a minute to talk. They were wearing white T-shirts and blue jeans. They had no coats and rain was on the way.

I told them they had better head for home, but they didn't want to turn back. It was Sunday, and Saturday night revelers had been generous with their cans and bottles. The sack was beginning to bulge and they wanted to fill it. They hurried on.

It got wild and windy after they left. When the rain came, it came all at once. It was a regular downpour. If I hadn't had raingear I would have headed for shelter.

In a little while the boys came back. "You're right," said one. "It sure is raining." They were soaked. Their hair was matted down and their T-shirts fit tight as skin. They shivered as they talked.

I told them they had better get in the barn until it let up, but they were headed for the little store down the road a quarter of a mile. That's where dreams come true when you've got a sackful of cans and bottles to cash in.

I watched them go, then I went back to work. After a while I realized that I felt differently. They had infected me with their bright-eyed enthusiasm. When I started whistling I became concerned.

The thought of enjoying something I've hated doing for so long was certainly cause for alarm. It had to be a sign of mental decay, and I have decayed about as far as I dare.

By concentrating, I got myself back into that dark-brown frame of mind that digging postholes should naturally arouse.

It was a good thing I was on the alert. If I hadn't been, those boys might have ruined what turned out to be a perfectly miserable afternoon.

Thoughts To Warm Fall Days

When frost touches the pumpkin and everything begins to wilt, I start thinking about stoves.

I'm not talking about the conventional models, those works of art all trimmed in chrome, with pretty handles and doors that should be hanging in art galleries. They are OK in their place, which is a living room much fancier than I'm used to.

Even the cook stoves are beginning to look nice, the way they come all decorated up. But I can't get excited about those dandified showpieces. They look too much like ornaments to me.

I go for stoves that are designed for utility -- and look like it. Usually they are painted black, and the smoke I've seen escape from them when the doors were opened could paint a ceiling the same color in no time.

Some of the more efficient models could even add a rich smoky tinge to the walls throughout most of the house. but you didn't often get one of them. They were classics.

Some were fine examples of pyrotechnical engineering. I especially like the top-loaders, the ones with the door that swung out over the side so you could look directly into the firebox to see how things were going.

If you had ball bearings for eyeballs, you could. Unfortunately, I was not so equipped and mine flooded out in teary rebellion when the first thick cloud of smoke hit them.

But you didn't have to look -- not once you got the feel of things. After a while you could tell by the blast that hit you when you opened the door how big a chunk of wood to drop in, while you shielded your face with your free hand.

Sometimes it was difficult to ignore the sparks that erupted when the wood hit the bottom of the firebox. They were especially had to ignore if they started smoking on a fine doily -- or a new sofa.

One stove we had surpassed all others when it came to personality. It was short and squat, with thin walls that rippled like running water after it had been used for a while.

It didn't take much fuel to turn the walls a bright, cherry red. If the stove was loaded with too much dry wood, they would turn an angry red the way an infected thumb does.

One evening it reached that color, and it kept spreading until the whole stove was red and sullen. You couldn't get within three feet of it without getting singed, and we were afraid it was going to melt down, then and there.

We didn't want to soak everything while trying to put the fire out with water, so we slipped a pair of long 2x4's under the stove and carried it out of the house. When the stovepipe pulled loose from the chimney, it released a shower of sparks that reminded me of the aurora borealis.

The stove protested with a hot scorching sound when we tossed it into the snow that covered the yard. But it didn't appear to be any the worse for wear when we carried it back into the house the next morning.

Moisture from melting snow had bleached the black off one side, which gave it a rather unique appearance. In a bloated sort of way, it resembled a Holstein calf.

One of the best stoves I ever saw was shaped like a big barrel laid on its side. It was equipped with a set of tubes that ran full length at the top where the heat collected.

It was used to heat an auction barn, and a big fan at the back forced air through the tubes. It would burn anything six feet in length, and it produced a hearty blast when it was fired up.

The tubes were about two inches in diameter, and when the fan was operating at top speed it was like standing in front of a dozen bazookas, all going off at once.

I heard one fellow say he would rather face a firing squad than that stove when it was going full blast. He knew what he was talking about, I can assure you.

When chill winds begin to blow, it's nice to have a few old stoves smoldering in your memory.

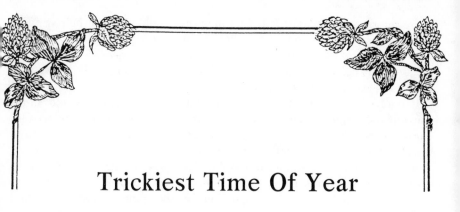

Trickiest Time Of Year

It seems to me that February comes at the wrong time of the year to do any good. I think it was just sort of squeezed in to make calendars long enough to display all those pretty pictures they are decorated with.

It reminds me of cracker crumbs some people put in hamburger to make it go farther. In a way, it's like adding water to fill up a gas tank. It looks better than it really is.

I'll admit, however, that if you need to be born about that time of year, February comes in handy. If we didn't have it, we wouldn't have two of our most famous men: George Washington and Abraham Lincoln.

Without February, I suppose they would have been out of luck. And I'll bet it would get a little uncomfortable going around unborn for the rest of your life.

That's the trouble with February. It puts kinks in people's lives. It's erratic, too. Every four years it adds another day, which throws some people completely out of time.

I have a friend who was born on February 29, and it has left him in a perpetual state of confusion. Since his birthday only comes once every four years, he's only 25 percent as old as he is.

If that's the case, he wants to know why he doesn't feel 75 percent younger than he does. But that's not all that disgruntles him. How, he asks, can he enjoy a second childhood when he can't get old enough to get out of the first one?

You've got to admit that he's got a point. It's not surprising that he's developed a complex. When you're way ahead of your age you naturally feel a little strange.

Of course, there's one day in February people might object to losing if the month were cancelled, as I'm proposing. Manufacturers of heart-shaped candies would no doubt protest.

But think how much less wear and tear bathroom scales would suffer if all

137

those calories were eliminated. And then they could save all their strength for Christmas when things get really weighty.

February is at its trickiest best -- or worst, I should say -- when it enlists the sun in its nefarious schemes, which it usually does for a week or two near the end of its 28 -- or 29 -- deceitful days.

It really raises Cain then. With all of that sudden, bright and sunny warmth it inveigles plants and flowers into thinking spring has arrived. Normally, they're too smart for that, but after enduring months of dark and drizzly grey they are willing to be misled.

It's actually more a matter of wishful thinking than anything else. They want to believe spring has arrived. If you've ever bought a pair of shoes because you liked their looks only to find that they pinched your feet, you'll understand that feeling.

But they're vulnerable, as old February knows. And just when they're beginning to shed their winter doldrums she drops the temperature from a high of 65 to a low of 22 and wilts them with a frost. If they come back later in the year looking sort of worried, worn and wary they have good reason.

Sometimes they don't come back at all. We've got flowers around the house that refuse to expose so much as a sprout anymore. If they could talk, I know they would say:

"As long as there's a February around,

"We're not coming out of the ground."

Despite all its drawbacks, February does us one good turn. It gets us out of January, which should be rescheduled for the middle of summer when it's not so cold and dreary.

The Fall Of The Last Leaf

On a quiet afternoon I watched autumn strip the oak trees of their leaves.

Lazily, without haste they came down, each one a leaf in summer's chapter coming to a close. But how differently they descended.

Some fell carefully, like commas expertly placed. Others floated aimlessly, I thought, like semicolons uncertain of their place. A few soared briefly the way I would expect an exclamation mark to soar. And there were those that fell straight down like periods ending a sentence.

Now it is another afternoon, and the wind is bustling through the trees beside the house to announce the coming of a storm. It is a big-shouldered wind, strong and steady as the mountains from which it blows.

It is rambunctious and unruly. It is a young and restless wind. It hasn't come to spend a quiet afternoon. It has come to have some fun.

It has no respect for leaves that have done their duty. It doesn't respect the old and weary, the rusty and the wrinkled. It surges with life -- with now, not yesterday.

With dignity, with the solemnity that befits the honored, leaves should be laid to rest. With care, I thought, they should gently be spread across the fields. They are veterans who have faithfully done their time.

But Nature holds no funerals. She expects everything to do its duty, then depart. If they fail to go, in time she will send them off for good.

So the wind came on that afternoon and stormed recklessly through the trees. And leaves that had hung so sedate and still spun off on their last journey.

They came tumbling out of the trees like startled wrens and crash landed in confusion. With an airy laughter the wind scuttled them against the fence.

Dignity is overcome by haste. It cannot be hurried. It is the slow, unhurried spiral a hawk unwinds against a summer sky. It is an elk strolling peacefully through evening's long drawnout shadows.

But dignity in haste becomes grace in a pigeon's rocketing flight. And it abounds in a deer's spring-loaded bounce across an open field.

Thus did some leaves fall on that afternoon. Despite the wind's irreverent puffery they would not be overcome. Gracefully they came down.

They contrasted sharply with those that departed in wild disorder, as soldiers do who bolt and run before an overwhelming enemy.

Some shot straight across the yard, unerring as an arrow. They would not be deflected by a wind that did not care. They would not be disgraced in their last flight.

And then came the nimble, those that remained light at heart even as they were whisked away forever. They bounced like buoys as they swirled, then soared high on an updraft's quick, sharp thrust to meet the wind that waited for them above the trees.

Some danced. They turned slowly in their one-way flight, as though entranced by some strange farewell melody. In three-quarter time they waltzed by like martyrs going to their doom.

If Mother Nature awarded Oscars, autumn would surely get one for best of show.

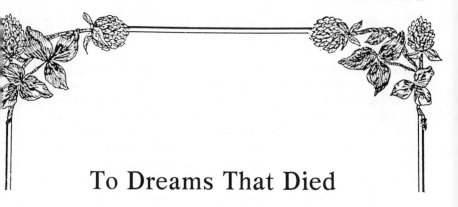

To Dreams That Died

How desolate they are, those old homesteads that stand in the desert empty and alone -- memorials to dreams that died before they could develop.

They are ghosts that linger around a door that never closes. They are shattered glass and a gate that sags on rusty hinges. And a three-legged table standing at an angle on a tilted floor, a chair with a broken back, and ragged paper peeling off rough board walls.

Abandoned homesteads in the desert are a past that didn't go away. They are haunted by lives that stayed a while, then went away.

And all around, in every direction, sagebrush and juniper jerk fitfully in a wind that lifted the cries of a lonely heart, that dried despairing tears and whispered sadly as it sniffed around a porch that sagged.

It is different in the desert where rains didn't come, where time no longer obeys the ticking of the clock, where yesterday melts with tomorrow into the silence of today.

Where rains arrive on schedule, abandoned homesteads never seem as deserted as they do in the desert that ripples in the distance like water in the sun.

There, where it is warm and moist, a wild, rank growth rushes in to fill the void. Before abandoned buildings can stand with dignified neglect, they have been subdued by tough, unruly invaders.

Soon grass crowds up close to a building it wasn't allowed to stand beside. It sneaks up through cracks in an old boardwalk. It comes to take back space it never intended to give away.

Then berry vines and briars begin to assert their claim. With wiry tendons they encircle, creep and climb to claw at windows where cobweb doilies hang.

Where rains come, old buildings become prey of a relentless foe camouflaged in natural green. It becomes a shroud in which buildings rot and ruin, crumple and collapse. With nothing left to hang onto, nails pull out and moss scabs over the crack in a brick that broke when a chimney fell.

What happened to the dream that built a house, that fixed a fence around a yard knee-deep in grass and set out a blood red rose? Where -- and when -- did the last petal fall?

Dreams that die in nature's fertile palm don't seem as poignant as those that linger in the desert under high, pale blue cloudless skies because death doesn't dress in growing green. It comes in somber, starker hues.

In the desert, old age stains the weathered wood with chocolate brown, warps it some and cracks it to the bone. It strips a corral of all its bark and tilts a weary post. In the desert, old age brands before it destroys.

With tired reserve old homesteads settle down like weary cattle. Somewhere along the line they strayed from the path that led to greener pastures.

The hand that drove the nails once reached with hope into a future that shimmered like a mirage before it dissolved. The nails held tight, but hope alone could not sustain a grasp that had nothing to hang onto.

In the desert, phantoms hover old homesteads that won't give up their ghosts.

Gifts We Never Count

Perhaps tonight, in the still darkness, in the unrushed luxury of an expiring Christmas Day, we should take inventory of the gifts we never count.

It would be an appropriate time, I think, before the new year begins to behold this strange, vast universe in which we exist because a power so great it defies slide rule and computer has allowed us to.

With the alarm clock's jangling demands hours away, contemplate for a moment the timeless mysteries that surround us on all sides. Take a trip deep in space, reach out in dim, dark distance without end, where the infinite makes a mockery of miles and meters.

In the hush of night peer into ravenous black holes, those great vacuums buried in space, so powerful they can warp time and space, or so the scientists say.

With a force so great they could reduce the planet Earth to football size, they overwhelm our capacity to comprehend. By such compression it is confounded.

Speed through cold, deep outer space. Soar through clouds of stars awash in misty solar light. And sail through 10 billion years that an indifferent cosmic calendar abandoned.

Then let your mind come drifting back. Let it relax, if it can after all it has seen, to ponder the mystery of it all. And such mystery.

Life, for instance, and why? Why life at all? And all of us and everything? What about that? And the silky fuzz of a peach?

In the quiet eddies of a Christmas Day about to end, wander among the engimas, where answers are more elusive than a flying star.

Space that refuses to end, and time that has become eternal, boggles the intellect. But we needn't travel far to contemplate what we cannot comprehend.

Consider the Earth, for instance, this planet, a sphere obeying commands

143

no one ever hears, the oasis of the universe, or so it seems: the spa of the solar system.

Like a ship adrift in a sea of meteoric derelicts it is revolving toward a destiny that cannot be perceived. And we with it -- all of us and everything included.

And what of that destiny? Will what's done here -- the good and the bad -- be weighed one against the other to determine whether the earth shall live or die?

Is it, and all the life upon it, some kind of celestial experiment as some suggest? Are we the architects of its survival, or do we inhabit to destroy?

Earth, The Miraculous, home for all the life we know of in the universe. So why, I wonder -- as I have so many times -- does it receive such shabby treatment? Shouldn't miracles be treated with more respect?

Through a haze of questions we wander, seeking, always searching. Through great billowing, mushrooming clouds we stumble as we strive to avoid the last deadend.

And we can. Another miracle points the way: that which occurred with the birth of Jesus Christ 2,000 years ago: He who lit the lamp of life for all mankind to see.

If we vow to, if we pledge on this Christmas Day to practice as He preached, perhaps we can begin to avoid the dreaded day -- "The Day After" -- and the haunting feeling that hope has forever been darkened by despair.

If there is still time for another miracle, this day -- this waning Christmas Day, could become a miracle that could save the Earth -- and all of us.

ABOUT THE AUTHOR

Jerry Easterling came late to the writing game. Although he received a degree in Journalism from the University of Oregon shortly after World War II, he spent the next 20 years doing the things that became fodder for the weekly column he began writing for the Statesman-Journal in 1977.

He worked as a logger, a sawmill hand, truck driver, carpenter, plus various other odd and unrelated jobs. But most of the time he was in the auction business, which he calls one of the "wildest businesses you could wind up in."

In addition to being an auctioneer, he was also a pitchman. For some time he traveled the five western states selling new merchandise at auction. Since 1970, he's been working for newspapers in Salem, Oregon. He is presently a feature writer and columnist for the Statesman-Journal. He, his wife Jeanne, and their family, live on a small farm in the foothills of the Coast Range Mountains, 32 miles west of Salem.